GREENBACK PLANET

Discovering
AMERICA
SERIES

Mark Crispin Miller, Editor

This series begins with a startling premise—that even now, more than two hundred years since its founding, America remains a largely undiscovered country with much of its amazing story yet to be told. In these books, some of America's foremost historians and cultural critics bring to light episodes in our nation's history that have never been explored. They offer fresh takes on events and people we thought we knew well and draw unexpected connections that deepen our understanding of our national character.

H. W. Brands

GREENBACK
PLANET

How the Dollar Conquered the World
and Threatened Civilization as We Know It

University of Texas Press
AUSTIN

Requests for permission to reproduce material from this work should be
sent to:
    Permissions
    University of Texas Press
    P.O. Box 7819
    Austin, TX 78713-7819
    www.utexas.edu/utpress/about/bpermission.html

⊚ The paper used in this book meets the minimum requirements of ANSI/
NISO Z39.48-1992 (R1997) (Permanence of Paper).

Library of Congress Cataloging-in-Publication Data

Brands, H. W.
    Greenback planet : how the dollar conquered the world and threatened
civilization as we know it / H. W. Brands. — 1st ed.
        p.   cm. — (Discovering America series)
    Includes index.
    ISBN 978-0-292-72341-2 (cloth : alk. paper) — ISBN 978-0-292-73579-8
(e-book)
    1. Dollar, American—History.   2. Monetary policy—United States.
3. International finance.   I. Title.
    HG501.B67   2011
    332.4′973—dc22   2011011982

≡ CONTENTS ≡

INTRODUCTION
- 1 -

Fiat Lucre: 1863–1907
- 4 -

Strong and Stronger: 1907–1928
- 25 -

Skulls and Bones: 1929–1944
- 42 -

The View from
Mount Washington: 1944–1963
- 60 -

Floating, Floating . . . : 1963–1973
- 75 -

Petrodollars, Eurodollars and the
Invincible Yen: 1973–1989
- 84 -

Bubble and Boil: 1990–2002
- 95 -

8

Be Nice to Your Creditors: 2003–
- 109 -

NOTES
- 125 -

ACKNOWLEDGMENTS
- 133 -

INDEX
- 135 -

GREENBACK PLANET

≡ INTRODUCTION ≡

On January 1, 1863, Abraham Lincoln signed the Emancipation Proclamation, freeing most of America's slaves. On March 3 of that year, he signed a revision of the Legal Tender Act, freeing the American dollar from its dependence on gold and silver. The first measure marked the demise of the system of political economy Americans had inherited from colonial days; the second signaled the launch of American capitalism toward global dominance.

The dollar had been America's official currency for decades, but it had always been chained to precious metal; by creating fiat money, backed only by the credit—and credibility—of the federal government, Lincoln made possible innovations in finance unimagined by previous generations. Some of these innovations would be felt at once, as the greenback underwrote the Union victory in the Civil War and accelerated America's industrial revolution. Other innovations would take longer, not least since stubborn tradition distrusted nonconvertible currency and continued to demand gold. Tradition compromised with innovation in the 1913 establishment of the Federal Reserve system, which allowed the government to fine-tune the nation's money supply.

The tuners, however, hit some bad notes, and when the

stock market crashed in 1929 the Fed failed to provide liquidity to prevent the stock swoon from spilling over into the broader economy. Dollars disappeared and prices plunged, until Franklin Roosevelt, in defiance of respectable opinion and international comity, did what the Fed couldn't and devalued the dollar. Roosevelt's isolationist monetary policy may have contributed to the coming of World War II, which had the paradoxical—considering its origins—effect of catapulting the United States to global military, political and financial leadership.

The dominion of the dollar, institutionalized at the Bretton Woods conference of 1944, served America well for two decades, but it was an inevitably wasting asset. Under the aegis of the dollar, the economies of Germany and Japan revived and eroded America's hegemony. By the early 1970s the Bretton Woods system had become unsustainable. Richard Nixon shocked the diplomatic world by going to China, but his jolt to the financial world—by ending the convertibility of the dollar to gold—had more sweeping and protracted effects. The dollar became merely the first among currency equals, floating like them on a sea of constantly changing worries and expectations.

Yet Nixon's forced-hand coup turned out to be a stroke of inadvertent genius. Medieval alchemists had long sought to turn lead into gold; the American president accomplished something more miraculous: turning paper to gold. By detaching the dollar from gold, Nixon made the greenback the fundamental standard of value in world finance. Other currencies could rise against the dollar, but the dollar's ubiquity, its ready convertibility into other currencies and its backing by what remained the most powerful economy on earth gave the dollar greater clout than ever in the markets of the world.

This became apparent almost at once, when the oil crises of the 1970s sent energy prices soaring. Americans paid the higher bills along with everyone else, but unlike everyone else they paid in their own currency. The "petrodollars" amassed by OPEC returned to America to finance a swelling federal deficit and the still-rising American standard of living. And when inflation in the United States hit record levels, it silently recaptured for Americans part of the oil price surge.

Events of the following decades reinforced the dollar's dominance. The collapse of communism left the American model of democratic capitalism as the only system most countries cared to emulate. The revolution in communications technology underpinned a globalization that sent dollars rocketing around the world at the speed of electrons. No single currency commanded the official allegiance of the entire planet, but the dollar came closer than any currency ever had.

Americans benefited from the dollar's reign, and so did the world—as long as markets rose and investment smiled. The 1990s were, by most measures, the best decade in world economic history. But when, several years into the new millennium, an international bubble in real estate burst, and when banks on six continents found themselves holding one another's bad debt, denominated mostly in dollars, the costs of the greenback's hegemony became apparent. Financial miscues that once had been confined to local or regional markets now roared around the planet like tsunamis, swamping individuals, firms and countries almost without warning. Credit markets crashed; otherwise healthy businesses found themselves bereft of the means to carry on. Hundreds of millions of people planet-wide lost their jobs. Countries with the largest dollar holdings—China most conspicuously—sought the safety of currency diversification but discovered that their efforts to diminish the danger risked making it worse.

After a harrowing year, the crisis eased. Financial markets regained a modicum of stability; the dollar emerged almost as essential as ever. But no serious observer believed that the danger had vanished. The next tremor might trigger another tsunami, producing even greater damage than before.

≡ FIAT LUCRE ≡

1863–1907

T he dollar became America's currency by historical happenstance. The silver mines of Mexico and Peru made Spain the envy of its imperial competitors during the sixteenth, seventeenth and eighteenth centuries, and Spanish silver dollars anchored the economies of the Americas and much of the rest of the world. Spanish dollars—the word *dolar* derived from the German *thaler*, an abbreviated reference to silver coins minted from metal dug from the ground at Joachimsthal in Bohemia—circulated in England's North American colonies at the time of the American Revolution, and when the Continental Congress chose a currency for the nascent republic it adopted the one Americans knew best. The independence of the Spanish dollar from the British government rendered it the more attractive to a people who had taken up arms against King George.

The federal constitution of 1787 granted the new Congress the power "to coin money" and "regulate the value thereof." The legislature exercised this power in the Coinage Act of 1792, which described the series of coins to be struck by the United States mint, based on "dollars or units: each to be of the value of a Spanish milled dollar as the same is now current, and to contain three hundred and seventy-one grains and four-sixteenths parts of a grain of pure, or four hundred and sixteen grains of standard silver." There were problems with the Coinage Act, starting with its implicit evaluation of "standard silver" versus pure silver and extending to a similar weighing of silver against gold. "Eagles," for instance, were defined as equaling ten dollars, or 247 4/8 grains of pure gold. This equation effectively specified a particular exchange rate between gold and silver. Whether the United States government would, or could, defend the stipulated rate in the face of the discovery of new gold and silver mines, the advancement of refining technology and the ebb and flow of international trade were questions the legislators left for a later day.

More immediately pressing was the fact that the gold and silver coins couldn't cover the currency needs of the new nation. Specie had always been scarce in America, causing the colonists to turn to substitutes. Indian wampum—strings of beads or shells—served in some places; deeds to land or claims on tobacco or cotton elsewhere. Merchants employed bills of credit; individuals drafted checks against their personal good names. Colonial legislatures issued paper notes. This last method enjoyed the authority of government, which could tax to pay its obligations, but it suffered from the ease with which paper money—in contrast to gold or silver, or, for that matter, land—could be multiplied. Governments under stress were tempted to print more notes, trading the long-term cost of devaluation for the short-term benefit of liquidity. As governments succumbed to the temptation, the long term grew shorter; during the Revolutionary War the phrase "not worth a Continental" summarized the devaluation that gutted the paper currency issued by the Continental Congress.

Alexander Hamilton addressed the problem as the first treasury secretary under the 1787 constitution. Hamilton proposed the establishment of a nationally chartered but privately owned bank, the Bank of the United States, which would issue bank notes that would circulate as currency. Hamilton's plan pleased creditors, who benefited from a strong dollar—one that purchased at least as much on repayment as when it was lent. His plan upset debtors, who benefited from a weak dollar. Hamilton's critics, including Thomas Jefferson, the champion of debt-strapped farmers, additionally objected that the Bank of the United States would mortgage the public interest to the personal interests of the bank's wealthy shareholders. Hamilton didn't deny the allegation; on the contrary, he contended that the public interest *required* an alignment of government with the interests of the wealthy. Hamilton defeated Jefferson, with the help of dozens of members of Congress who became charter shareholders of the bank. The bank began operations in 1791 with a scheduled lifespan of twenty years.

By the time the bank's charter ran out in 1811, the Jeffersonians controlled the government, and they let the bank lapse. They soon wished they hadn't. The War of 1812 demonstrated the value of a stable currency and the convenience of a national bank, and in 1816 Jefferson's heirs rechartered the Bank of the United States for another twenty years. John Marshall and the Supreme Court eliminated lingering questions about the bank's constitutionality in the 1819 case of *McCulloch v. Maryland*.

Or so they thought. Andrew Jackson disagreed. Jackson held a belief common among his fellow Tennesseans and other westerners that the strong-dollar policies of the bank unfairly inhibited western growth. He held another belief, common throughout the country at the time, that although the Supreme Court spoke for the judicial branch of the government, it didn't speak for the executive or the legislature. Jackson had no compunctions about brushing aside Marshall's assertion of the bank's constitutionality; he contended that neither the expressed nor implied powers of the constitution authorized the charter of such a corporate monopoly.

Yet Jackson would have allowed the bank to expire peacefully when its charter ran out had the bank's backers not forced his hand. Henry Clay, with his eye on the 1832 election, got bank president Nicholas Biddle to request early recharter and Congress to deliver it. Jackson riposted with a veto of the

recharter bill. Jackson declared the bank not merely unconstitutional but dangerous to democracy. "When the laws undertake to . . . make the rich richer and the potent more powerful,
the humble members of society—the farmers, mechanics, and
laborers—who have neither the time nor the means of securing like favors to themselves, have a right to complain," Jackson said. "There are no necessary evils in government. Its evils
exist only in its abuses. If it would confine itself to equal pro-
tection, and, as Heaven does its rains, shower its favors alike
on the high and the low, the rich and the poor, it would be an
unqualified blessing." The Bank of the United States was no
blessing, but a curse.

Having eliminated the bank's future, Jackson proceeded
to dismantle its present. The bank's principal customer was
the federal government, whose huge deposits provided the
reserves against which the bank issued loans. Jackson ordered
the deposits removed from the bank and placed in various state
banks. Nicholas Biddle fought the removal, recalling loans and
otherwise tightening credit in ways intended to arouse public
opinion against the president. Jackson understood Biddle's
strategy and swore to defeat it. "The Bank, Mr. Van Buren, is
trying to kill me," he told his vice president. *"But I will kill it!"*

Jackson did kill the bank, defeating Biddle and vindicating
the principle that the representatives of the people, rather than
a small class of wealthy financiers, should direct the financial
fortunes of America. It was a great victory for democracy—and
a disaster for the economy. The bank's demise inaugurated an
orgy of speculation in land, funded by the flimsy credit of hundreds of poorly managed state banks; after Jackson curtailed
the gambling by requiring, in the Specie Circular of 1836, that
purchasers of federal lands pay with gold and silver, the economy froze up in the panic of 1837.

Not till the 1840s did the country recover, amid the enthu-
siasms of Manifest Destiny. Americans of the mid-
nineteenth century convinced themselves that Providence

smiled on them and their efforts to expand democracy west to the Pacific and south into Mexico. The annexation of Texas reflected this vision; it also triggered a war with Mexico, which continued to claim Texas. The war lasted two years and ended with American forces occupying Mexico City and its environs, including the village of Guadalupe Hidalgo, where a treaty transferring the northern half of Mexico to the United States, in exchange for a fig leaf payment of $15 million, was concluded.

At the time of the signing none of the negotiators realized that the most important financial discovery of the nineteenth century had just been made in part of the territory about to be transferred. In the foothills of the Sierra Nevada of California, above the trading post of John Sutter at the confluence of the American and Sacramento Rivers, an American expatriate named James Marshall discovered a gold nugget, followed by many others just like it. Marshall and Sutter tried to suppress the news, which nonetheless leaked out, inspiring a rush of global dimensions to California. Hundreds of thousands of miners scoured the streambeds and hillsides of the Sierra before plunging into the earth in pursuit of the ore-bearing veins. American gold production soared from less than $1 million annually to more than $50 million. The gold geology of California taught prospectors to find deposits elsewhere in the American West and around the world; the world's gold supply doubled during the next generation.

The glut of gold allowed other countries to follow the lead of Britain, which had tied its currency to gold some decades before. Britain's gold standard supported the expansion of British trade in such formal possessions as India, Australia and Canada, but also in the informal empire the British were creating in Central and South America. The United States didn't join the gold group formally, instead retaining the trappings of bimetallism. Yet the excess of gold compared to silver drove the latter out of circulation as debtors paid their bills in the relatively less valuable yellow metal. In 1853 Congress acknowledged the existing state of affairs and limited silver as legal tender—money that creditors were required to accept—to debts of five dollars or less. The result was a de facto gold standard.

The country experienced another panic, in 1857, after speculation in railroads and mining stocks turned sour and the *Central America*, a ship carrying $2 million in California gold to New York, went down in a hurricane off the Carolina coast. The financial panic intensified the fear many felt for the American republic, which was careening toward secession and civil war. The election of Abraham Lincoln furnished South Carolina the occasion for finally doing what inhabitants of the Palmetto State had been threatening to do for decades: bolt the Union. South Carolina's secession prompted similar actions by several other states, and when Lincoln forcibly resisted at Fort Sumter, the war began.

Wars are always expensive and typically test a belligerent's financial prudence and stamina. The infant American republic had failed the test during the Revolutionary War, staggering to victory only with infusions of French cash. The War of 1812 made the Jeffersonians believers in the concept of a national bank. But the Civil War was a sterner test than anyone had dreamed before the conflict started. The Confederacy failed even more dismally than the early American republic had; lacking both restraint and a foreign underwriter, the Confederate government printed reams of money that rapidly grew worthless.

The Union fared much better. The northern economy was stronger than that of the South; the population was larger and more productive. The North could stand tax increases to pay for war materiel, and Northerners bought government bonds in quantities that made Jefferson Davis drool.

Even so, the cost of the war outran the Union government's ability to tax and borrow. By early 1862 Salmon P. Chase, Lincoln's treasury secretary, concluded that continuing the war required taking the Union partway down the path the Confederacy was following. Chase proposed an issue of treasury notes unredeemable in gold or silver yet legal tender nonetheless.

Creditors were the first to complain, on the obvious ground that they had lent hard money but would receive flimsy in return. Their spokesmen in Congress decried the unfairness of this as well as its dubious constitutionality. Article 1 of the constitution authorized Congress to *coin* money, but nothing was said about *printing* money. This wasn't an oversight: the framers all bore painful memories of the devastating inflation spawned by the printed Continental dollars. Quite apparently they hadn't intended for Congress to crank up the printing presses again.

The advocates of the administration's bill promised that this time the printers—that is, the administration itself—would be circumspect. Paper money became a problem only when it proliferated; kept within bounds, it would lubricate commerce without depriving anyone of honest recompense.

The opponents weren't buying. In a rowdy debate they pounded the administration for lax morality and shady politics. "To make these notes legal tender for debts, private and public, contracted before the passage of the bill, seems to me a clear breach of good faith," Benjamin Franklin Thomas of Massachusetts told the House of Representatives. "Debts are obligations or promises to pay money. . . . Paper *is not money.*" Thomas didn't question the need to support the troops, but he wanted the administration to do so more forthrightly. "Take from us, Mr. Chairman, our property, houses, and lands; they cannot be devoted to a nobler cause. But in God's name leave us the consciousness of integrity; leave us our self-respect."

Owen Lovejoy of Illinois wanted the administration to acknowledge that it was playing loose with the constitution. "I would admit the plea of necessity, if I believed it," Lovejoy said. "And I think it is more manly to confess, as Jefferson did [in the Louisiana Purchase], that the thing was necessary but unconstitutional, than it is to attempt to torture the constitution into the support of a measure which everybody must see to be unconstitutional." Lovejoy likened the question of paper money to the theological doctrine of transubstantiation, by which bread and wine were transformed into the body and blood of Christ. "Believe that this piece of paper is a five-dollar gold piece, and it is a five-dollar gold piece," he mocked. "Believe it is worth five dollars, and it is worth five dollars." He didn't accept transubstantiation, and he wouldn't accept paper money. "It is not in the power of this Congress, nor in the power of any legislative body, to accomplish an impossibility in making something out of nothing." Lovejoy couldn't believe the government would be as self-denying as the administration promised. "When we have issued $100 million we must issue another $100 million, and then another $100 million. And thus we plunge from lower depth to still lower, till we are buried in an ocean of inconvertible paper." Shifting metaphors slightly, Lovejoy forecast imminent doom: "Sir, there is no precipice, there is no chasm, there is no possible yawning gulf before this nation so terrible, so appalling, so ruinous as this bill that is before us."

The supporters of the legal tender bill rallied to its defense. Thaddeus Stevens of Pennsylvania, the chairman of the House ways and means committee, asked Salmon Chase to write a letter explaining the treasury's thinking. Chase responded by confessing his own reservations about the bill. "I have felt, nor do I wish to conceal that I now feel, a great aversion to making anything but coin a legal tender in payment of debts," the secretary wrote. He said he had hoped to persuade people to accept government notes voluntarily. Many did so. "But, unfortunately, there are some persons and some institutions which refuse to receive and pay them, and whose action tends not merely to the unnecessary depreciation of the notes but to establish discriminations in business against those who, in this matter, give a cordial support to the government, and in favor of those who do not." For this reason the issue of the notes as legal tender had become "indispensably necessary."

Chase's explanation inspired other Republicans. "The bill before us is a war measure—a measure of *necessity*, and not of choice," Elbridge Spaulding of New York said. "These are extraordinary times, and extraordinary measures must be resorted to in order to save our government and preserve our nationality."

Charles Sumner of Massachusetts articulated the view that ultimately carried the day. "Surely we must all be against paper money," Sumner told the Senate. "We must all insist upon maintaining the integrity of the government, and we must all set our faces against any proposition like the present, except as a temporary expedient, rendered imperative by the exigency of the hour. . . . Your soldiers in the field must be paid and fed. Here there can be no failure or postponement. A remedy which at another moment you would reject is now proposed. Whatever may be the national resources, they are not now within reach except by summary process. Reluctantly, painfully, I consent that the process should issue."

The Legal Tender Act of 1862 authorized the treasury to issue $150 million in notes—which would be printed in green ink: hence the name "greenbacks"—that would be "lawful money and a legal tender in payment of all debts public and private," except for import duties and interest on federal bonds. A link to the past and to gold still existed: the treasury notes could be converted to federal bonds, which were backed by gold. But this link was severed at the next session of Congress, when the legislature specified nonconvertible notes and ordered holders of the old notes to redeem them by July 1, 1863. "Thereafter the right so to exchange the same shall cease," the new law said.

With this the greenback became pure fiat money: currency backed not by anything material but only by the promise of government not to abuse the printing privilege—and by the willingness of dollar-holders to suspend their disbelief in such promises. Considering the duress of the war, the two parties to the deal—the government and the dollar-holders—held up their ends of the bargain reasonably well. The value of the greenback declined against gold but did nothing like the vanishing act of the Continental dollar. During 1862 the greenback slid against gold until 129 greenback dollars were required to purchase 100 gold dollars. The greenback continued to drop during the spring of 1863, to 152 against 100 in gold, but after the Union victory at Gettysburg in July, the greenback recovered to 131. It slumped again during 1864, as Ulysses Grant made little progress against Robert E. Lee near Richmond; the low point came in July, when gold traded at 258. By the time of Lee's surrender to Grant in April 1865 the greenback had climbed to 150.

The rise and fall of the greenback against gold was part of an institutionalizing pattern of speculation. "Along with ordinary happenings, we fellows in Wall Street had the fortunes of war to speculate about," Daniel Drew, one of the most active speculators, recalled. "That always makes great doings on a stock exchange. It's good fishing in troubled waters." The fish pond for gold took shape informally, with traders initially conducting business at the edge of the stock exchange, then moving to a coal cellar on William Street, before winding up in a special venue, the Gold Room, on New Street beside the stock exchange. As the trading of gold for greenbacks became more intense, the atmosphere in the Gold Room grew less savory. "Imagine a rat-pit in full blast, with twenty or thirty men arranged around the rat tragedy, each with a canine under his arm, yelling and howling at once," journalist Horace White wrote. "The furniture of the room is extremely simple. It consists of two iron railings and an indicator." The indicator showed the current price of gold. "In the interior, which represents the space devoted to rat killing in other establishments, is a marble Cupid throwing up a jet of pure Croton water"—a source of civic pride for New Yorkers. "The artistic conception is not appropriate. Instead of a Cupid throwing a pearly fountain into the air there should have been a hungry Midas turning everything to gold and starving to death from inability to eat it."

As active as the gold-and-greenback trading was during the war, it became still more so in the years just after the conflict.

The accelerating growth of the American economy and the revival of international commerce following the Union victory spurred the demand for gold—to pay import duties, settle international accounts and hedge against fluctuations in the greenback—even as the government debated whether to retire the greenbacks and return to gold. The demand and the debate drove speculation to new levels. In 1869 an unlikely pair of speculators hatched an audacious plan to corner the gold market: to acquire more contracts to deliver gold than the market could sustain, and thereby force the contractors to accept what terms the pair dictated. Jay Gould was considered the Mephistopheles of Wall Street; Jim Fisk the P. T. Barnum. Gould, dark of eye and black of beard, silently laid the plans for the coup, craftily cutting certain members of the Grant administration in on the deal; Fisk, florid of face and full of voice, bellowed to the world that gold must go higher.

The critical moment occurred in late September 1869. The arrow in the Gold Room showed a price of 140. The price seemed higher than market conditions warranted; many speculators became gold bears, selling borrowed gold in anticipation of a fall in the price. Fisk led the gold bulls, trying to push the price higher. "The bear party at times seemed to be perfectly frantic while undergoing punishment at the hands of the exultant and defiant bulls," a journalist recorded. "And as the roar of battle and the screams of the victims resounded through New Street, it seemed as though human nature was undergoing torments worse than any that Dante ever witnessed in hell."

Things grew only worse for the bears. On the morning of Friday, September 24, the gold price lurched upward even before trading officially started. At the ten o'clock opening the indicator jumped from 143 to 150. "Take all you can get!" Fisk ordered his brokers. The price leaped to 155. "Take all you can get at 160!" The bears, who stood to lose millions, ran about the Gold Room bewailing their imminent demise. Some threatened mortal harm to the bulls. "Terror became depicted on every countenance," an eyewitness related. "Even those who had but little or no interest at stake were seized with the infection of fear and were conscious of a great evil approaching."

And then the market broke. Grant's treasury had watched the rise of gold but hadn't intervened, preferring to let the market find its own level. Yet as Gould and Fisk neared control of the market, and as the soaring gold price threatened to paralyze the nation's financial sector and perhaps derange the entire economy, Grant gave the order to act. The treasury's vaults in New York held enough gold to break any corner, and just before noon on that Friday a telegram arrived from Washington ordering the release of the treasury gold.

The news found its way to the Gold Room ahead of the official announcement. The price had passed 160; buyers were bidding 162. "A quiet voice said, 'Sold one million at 162,'" an observer recounted. But there were no other offers to purchase at that price. A broker bid 161 and found a seller. But that bid wasn't renewed. Another broker offered 160 for five million of gold. "Then it dimly dawned on the quicker witted that for some reason or other the game was up. As if by magnetic sympathy the same thought passed through the crowd at once. A dozen men leapt furiously at the bidder, and claimed to have sold the whole five millions. To their horror, the bidder stood his ground and declared he would take all. But before the words had fairly passed his lips, before the terror at his action had had time to gain men's hearts, there was a rush amid the crowd. New men, wild with fresh excitement, crowded to the barriers. In an instant the rumor was abroad: the treasury is selling." The end of the corner had come, with a vengeance. "All who had bought were mad to sell at any price, but there were no buyers. In less time than it takes to write about it, the price fell from 162 to 135. The great gigantic bubble had burst, and half Wall Street was involved in ruin."

The panic provoked by the events of Black Friday, as that September 24 was soon called, revived demands to retire the greenback and refix the dollar to gold. The move gained impetus from a surprising Supreme Court decision declaring the paper money unconstitutional. The surprising part of the decision wasn't the result, given the doubts that had surrounded the Legal Tender Act from the start, but its authorship. Salmon Chase had never warmed to Lincoln, nor Lincoln to him, and the president began looking for ways to rid himself of the treasury secretary. When Chief Justice Roger Taney died in 1864, Lincoln shifted Chase to the Supreme Court, where the new chief justice had a chance to reflect on his role in creating the greenback and to determine that such authority as the war had conferred on the government to substitute paper for gold-secured money had expired with the war's end. The power to print money wasn't what the framers had wished to grant Congress, Chase asserted on behalf of the court's majority in the 1870 case of *Hepburn v. Griswold*. "It is certainly not the same power as the power to coin money. Nor is it in any reasonable or satisfactory sense an appropriate or plainly adapted means to the exercise of that power." The legal tender law, moreover, altered the terms of contracts without the consent of the parties. "No one will question that the United States notes, which the act makes a legal tender in payment, are essentially unlike in nature and, being irredeemable in coin, are necessarily unlike in value, to the lawful money intended by parties to contracts for the payment of money made before its passage." Therefore the law and the greenbacks were unconstitutional.

The verdict threatened American finance with anarchy, for it called into question nearly every contract written since 1862. But while the nation's lawyers were clearing their litigation calendars and counting the fees they would garner, Ulysses Grant rode to the rescue. The president filled two empty seats on the court with judges who found paper money acceptable, and the reconfigured court overturned the Hepburn decision. The final verdict of the bundled Legal Tender Cases, concluded in 1871, was that Congress *could* print money. The greenback survived.

But it didn't thrive. In 1873 Congress passed a new Coinage Act, which omitted the silver dollar from the list of authorized coins. A "trade dollar"—intended for foreign commerce—was included, and silver coins of smaller denominations, but not the silver dollar allowed since the early days of the republic. The omission would shortly be damned as the "crime of '73," an alleged conspiracy against the interest of ordinary Americans. But at the moment it merely reflected the continuing dearth of silver compared to gold. Many Americans in the early 1870s had never seen a silver dollar and had to be told what they were missing.

More important at the time was the matter of "resumption"—the resuming of the specie convertibility of all dollars. In the autumn of 1873 a bubble in railroad stocks burst, provoking a panic that yielded calls for a return to sounder finance. Congress responded in 1875 with the Resumption Act, which ordered the retirement of greenbacks starting in 1879. At that point the country would be on the road back to the gold standard.

By then, though, a countercurrent had set in. The business depression that followed the 1873 panic caused farm prices to slump. Other prices fell, too, but farmers, chronically dependent on debt to pay for equipment, seed and labor in advance of the post-harvest sale of their crops, regularly found themselves repaying yesterday's costly borrowing with today's meager revenues. They and their spokesmen sought relief through re-inflation, which they hoped to accomplish by an increase in the money supply. Their plan was to return the nation's money system to its bimetallic roots, and their cry was "Free silver at 16 to 1," meaning the unrestrained coining of all the silver delivered to the mint, at the generous ratio of sixteen ounces of silver to one of gold.

The silver forces made headway with the 1878 passage of the Bland-Allison Act, which reintroduced the silver dollar. They gathered momentum during the 1880s under the banner of the Farmers Alliance, which vigorously endorsed silver.

They sponsored the 1890 Sherman Silver Purchase Act, which injected additional silver into the currency system.

Their progress inspired the establishment of the Populist Party, which agitated for free silver and other causes close to the hearts of farmers. But it frightened foreign investors, who feared the devaluation of the American dollar. Untimely stumbles by key railroad and banking companies spooked British dollar-holders, who demanded gold in exchange. A panic ensued in the spring of 1893, producing the worst depression in American history to date, with hundreds of banks and thousands of other firms collapsing and millions of workers losing their jobs.

The dollar nearly broke under the strain. The treasury's gold reserve plunged, testing the $100 million floor set by statute and deemed by Wall Street essential to the government's ability to function. The plunge grew steeper: the faster the gold reserve dwindled, the more dollars were delivered for redemption.

In early 1895 the situation grew critical. The reserve fell through $100 million to $68 million on January 24, to $45 million on January 31 and to $10 million on February 2. All evidence indicated that within days, perhaps hours, the dollar would be broken and the United States driven off the gold standard.

Grover Cleveland turned to the one man who might save the day. The president approached J. P. Morgan gingerly; most of Cleveland's fellow Democrats loathed Morgan and all the titan of finance stood for. But Morgan commanded the confidence of the financial markets and could stem the run on the dollar, if anyone could. And Morgan was willing to try. Patriotism shaped his thinking: he didn't want to see America's currency collapse any more than the rest of the country did. But profits counted equally: Morgan's investments were nearly all in dollars, and if the dollar broke, he'd suffer more than most.

He traveled from the nation's financial capital to its political capital in his private rail car. "I have come down to Washington to see the President," he announced. Cleveland indicated a preference for indirect dealing. Morgan wouldn't be put off. "I am going to stay here until I see him," he insisted.

Cleveland consented. He brought Morgan to the White House and explained the parlous condition of the nation's fisc. Morgan replied that the president didn't know the worst of it. Morgan said that a single investor held a draft of $10 million against the treasury's gold. "If that $10 million draft is presented, you can't meet it," Morgan said. "It will be all over."

Cleveland asked Morgan what he could do.

Morgan vetoed a public bond offering, which some in the government had suggested. A public offering would require days to prepare; the dollar would be dead by then. A private bond sale would be swifter. Morgan offered to guarantee the sale, speaking for himself and a syndicate of investors. Cleveland questioned the legality of a private deal. Morgan had researched the matter and he referred to a Civil War statute, never repealed, that allowed the president to purchase gold coin with United States bonds "upon such terms as he may deem most advantageous to the public interest." Cleveland looked to John Carlisle, his treasury secretary, who checked Morgan's reference. "That seems to fit the situation exactly," Carlisle said.

Morgan wanted Cleveland to buy $100 million in gold from his syndicate; Cleveland, worried about being seen as Morgan's minion, said $60 million would have to do. The president asked for assurance that the deal would, in fact, save the dollar. "Mr. Morgan, what guarantee have we that if we adopt this plan, gold will not continue to be shipped abroad, and while we are getting it in, it will go out, and we will not reach our goal? Will you guarantee that this will not happen?"

Morgan didn't hesitate. "Yes, sir," he said. "I will guarantee it during the life of the syndicate, and that means until the contract has been concluded and the goal has been reached."

Morgan proved as good as his word and as bad as Cleveland's fears. The Morgan deal saved the dollar but provoked an uproar among Democrats who demanded to know what Morgan's profit was. He refused to say, even when brought before a congressional investigative committee. The affair weakened the gold wing of the Democratic Party and primed the 1896 national convention to listen when a young, pro-silver orator from Nebraska, William Jennings Bryan, strode onto the stage at Chicago. "Some men are so ugly and ungainly that it is a positive advantage to them as public speakers," a delegate recorded. "Some are so handsome and graceful that they are on good terms with the audience before they open their lips. Of the latter class Bryan is a shining example. His appearance is a passport to the affections of his fellow men which all can read. He is the picture of health: mental, moral, and physical. He stands about 5 feet 10, weighs about 170, is a pronounced brunette, has a massive head, a clean-shaven face, an aquiline nose, large under-jaw, square chin, a broad chest, large lustrous dark eyes, a mouth extending almost from ear to ear, teeth white as pearls, and hair—what there is left of it—black as midnight."

Many of the delegates fell for Bryan as soon as he took the stage. Others, committed to gold and the soundness of the dollar, determined to resist. To them Bryan spoke gently at first but soon with the passion of America's farmers and others who struggled to pay their debts. "When you come before us and tell us that we shall disturb your business interests, we reply that you have disturbed *our* business interests," he said. "The farmer who goes forth in the morning and toils all day, begins in the spring and toils all summer, and by the application of brain and muscle to the natural resources of this country creates wealth, is as much a business man as the man who goes upon the Board of Trade and bets upon the price of grain."

The delegates began to rock to the rhythm of Bryan's words. Handkerchiefs drawn to wipe damp foreheads now waved salutes to the speaker. Bryan professed no animus against the defenders of gold and the creditor classes, yet neither did he yield anything to them. "We do not come as aggressors," he said. "Our war is not a war of conquest. We are fighting in defense of our homes, our families and posterity. We have petitioned, and our petitions have been scorned. We have entreated, and our entreaties have been disregarded. We have begged, and they have mocked, and our calamity came. We beg no longer. We entreat no more. We petition no more. We defy them!"

The audience was in Bryan's palm. He slowed his pace to review the recent history of the dollar. He claimed for the people the right of government to issue money in the manner that best suited the people's needs. He contrasted two concepts of government. The elitist view contended that if legislation made the wealthy more prosperous, their prosperity would trickle down upon those below. Bryan took the opposite, democratic view. "The democratic idea has been that if you legislate to make the masses prosperous their prosperity will find its way up and through every class." The gold men put themselves on the side of the cities against the country; Bryan swept his arm and the imagination of his audience toward the open prairies beyond Chicago. "I tell you that the great cities rest upon these broad and fertile prairies. Burn down your cities and leave our farms, and your cities will spring up again as if by magic. But destroy our farms, and the grass will grow in the streets of every city in this country."

The fight for the dollar was the struggle for self-government, Bryan said. The gold men bowed to foreign bankers. "It is the issue of 1776 all over again. Our ancestors, when but three millions, had the courage to declare their political independence of every other nation upon earth. Shall we, their descendants, when we have grown to seventy millions, declare that we are less independent than our forefathers?" The gage was cast, the battle lines drawn. "If they dare to come out and in the open defend the gold standard as a good thing, we shall fight them to the uttermost, having behind us the producing masses of this nation and the world." Bryan held his arms out straight to either side, his face shining with sweat and the glow of righteousness. "We shall answer their demands for a gold standard by saying to them, 'You shall not press down upon the brow of labor this crown of thorns! You shall not crucify mankind upon a cross of gold!'"

Bryan's oratorical brilliance made him the Democrats' nominee and the dollar the central issue of the 1896 campaign. His pro-silver platform promised to weaken the dollar, that debtors might benefit from higher prices; the gold platform of Republican nominee William McKinley defended the dollar's strength, to preserve the position of creditors and the honor and liquidity of the government. Bryan campaigned heroically but in vain; Americans proved to be more conservative in money matters than Bryan and the silverites hoped. McKinley won handily, and before his first term ended he and Congress made explicit what his electoral victory implied. "The dollar consisting of twenty-five and eight-tenths grains of gold, nine-tenths fine," the Gold Standard Act of 1900 declared, "shall be the standard unit of value, and all forms of money issued or coined by the United States shall be maintained at a parity of value with the standard."

The gold law, which entailed a gold price of $20.67 per troy ounce, settled the question of what the dollar consisted of. Silver was out; paper was out; gold alone made a dollar. The United States joined the other industrialized countries on the gold standard.

But the gold law couldn't guarantee what the dollar was supposed to secure: room for the economy to grow without getting out of control. Another panic threatened the financial markets in 1907 after speculation in copper stocks boomeranged and brought down the Knickerbocker Trust Company, one of Wall Street's largest firms. Firms linked to the Knickerbocker wobbled, shareholders shuddered and the nation braced for a bust.

Theodore Roosevelt liked J. P. Morgan even less than Grover Cleveland had, despite being a Republican. Yet Roosevelt too felt obliged to turn to the powerful financier. He sent his treasury secretary to New York to enlist Morgan's support in stemming the panic, and he promised government funding for the bailout.

Morgan was slow to respond, having contracted a cold some days before. "Mr. Morgan could not be waked up," Herbert Satterlee, Morgan's son-in-law and business associate, recalled of a morning amid the crisis, when New York and the nation looked anxiously to the great banker. "If he could not be aroused, the consequences were too serious to contemplate." But Morgan eventually did wake up, and he threw himself into the breach. "Anyone who saw Mr. Morgan going from the Clearing House back to his office that day will never forget the picture," Satterlee continued. "With his coat unbuttoned and flying open, a piece of white paper clutched tightly in his right hand, he walked fast down Nassau Street. His flat-topped black derby hat was set firmly down on his head. Between his teeth he held a paper cigar holder in which was one of his long cigars, half-smoked. His eyes were fixed straight ahead. He swung his arms as he walked and took no notice of anyone. He did not seem to see the throngs in the street, so intent was his mind on the thing that he was doing. . . . He was the embodiment of power and purpose."

Morgan summoned the heads of New York's banking houses to a series of meetings at his library. The bankers thrashed out rescue plans in the library's east wing while Morgan played solitaire in the west wing. Periodically they sent plans across the marbled hall that separated the wings; he glanced up from his cards at the plans and told the bankers to try again. The duress wore the participants down. Benjamin Strong of Bankers' Trust fell asleep on a sofa on Saturday night, November 2; James Stillman of National City Bank, sitting next to him, asked when he had last been to bed. "Thursday night," Strong answered. Strong stirred himself sufficiently to present to Morgan what the bankers hoped would be their last proposal. Strong spoke his piece and tried to go home, only to discover that Morgan had locked the library doors. No one could leave until the crisis had been resolved.

Morgan eventually had to impose a deal. He crossed the hall to the bankers' room, holding a schedule according to which each man's firm would put up a portion of the $25 million Morgan judged necessary to hold the system together. One of his lawyers read the document to the exhausted financiers. "There you are, gentlemen," he said.

No one volunteered to sign first.

Morgan placed his hand on the shoulder of Edward King, head of Union Trust and the dean, after Morgan, of the money men. "There's the place, King. And here's the pen."

King did as Morgan directed. The other bankers followed. The danger passed.

≡ STRONG AND STRONGER ≡

1907–1928

Morgan thought his performance in the panic of 1907 should have earned him the thanks of the American people, or at least their respect. But he had thought the same thing about his role in stemming the run on the dollar in 1895, and he wasn't surprised that he became more unpopular than ever. The dollar now rested squarely on gold, making it sounder than it had been in decades, and Morgan had done as much as anyone to render that perch possible. But the very power that made him the dollar's principal custodian earned him the distrust of American progressives, who held the balance of political power in the country during the early twentieth century. They blamed Morgan for the creation of a "money trust," a web of interlocking boards and directorates said to monopolize American money and credit.

The assertion wasn't outlandish. Trusts dominated most sectors of the American economy, and several crucial ones were Morgan's doing. The biggest trust was United States Steel, the world's first billion-dollar corporation, crafted by Morgan in 1901 from holdings of Andrew Carnegie and John D. Rockefeller, among others. The Northern Securities railroad trust, another Morgan production, had so thoroughly controlled rail traffic in the northern tier of states that Theodore Roosevelt felt obliged to bring an antitrust suit against it. The suit succeeded but set the trust movement back only a little. Morgan continued to extend his reach, placing friends and associates on the boards of directors of banks and other corporations, till hardly a dollar changed hands, it often seemed, without Morgan's approval. His rescue of the banking system in 1907 simply publicized his strength, and evoked calls that it be curtailed.

Roosevelt's retirement from the White House—to hunt big game in Africa, causing Morgan, it was said on Wall Street, to propose a toast: "To the lions!"—delayed the enactment of the progressive agenda. But after new progressive gains in the 1910 elections, the House of Representatives appointed an investigative committee, headed by Arsène Pujo of Louisiana, to probe the money trust. Morgan was the star witness.

Morgan rarely spoke in public, and the prospect of the financial giant on the witness stand titillated the country. The committee room was packed with reporters, elected officials and whoever else could squeeze in. The chief counsel for the committee, Samuel Untermyer, had skewered lesser magnates than Morgan, employing knowledge he had gained in thirty years' corporate practice effecting mergers much like those on which he now grilled Morgan.

"You are an advocate of combination and cooperation, against competition, are you not?" Untermyer asked—or accused: even his blandest question had an edge to it.

"Yes, cooperation I should favor," Morgan replied, before adding: "I do not object to competition, either. I like a little competition."

"You like a little, if it does not hurt you?"

"I do not mind it." Morgan hesitated. "Now, another point. This may be a sensitive subject. I do not want to talk of it. This is probably the only chance I will have to speak of it."

"You mean the subject of combination and concentration?"

"Yes, the question of control. Without you have control, you cannot do anything."

"Is that the reason you want to control everything?" Untermyer fixed Morgan with a stare.

"I want to control nothing."

"What is the point, Mr. Morgan, you want to make?"

"What I say is this, that control is a thing, particularly in money, and you are talking about a money control—now, there is nothing in the world that you can make a trust on money."

"What you mean is that there is no way one man can get it all?"

"Or any of it. Or control of it."

"He can make a try of it?"

"No, sir, he cannot. He may have all the money in Christendom, but he cannot do it."

Untermyer asked Morgan about the influence he wielded on the broader economy. Morgan had designed the largest trusts; his partners and associates sat on their boards. Surely that gave him great power.

Morgan shook his head. He denied possessing the power Untermyer ascribed to him, or any substantial power at all. Neither did he want power.

Untermyer professed surprise. "You do not think you have any power in any department of industry in this country?" he said.

"I do not," Morgan answered.

"Not the slightest?"

"Not the slightest."

"You are not looking for any?"

"I am not seeking it, either."

Why then did he build the trusts as he did? "It is for the purpose of concentrating the interests that you amalgamate, is it not?"

"If it is desirable, yes," Morgan admitted, before thinking of a more politic answer: "If it is good business for the interests of the country."

Untermyer asked Morgan whether he considered it a duty to his clients to fend off their competition. When Morgan denied that he did, Untermyer pressed: "Then you consider your firm, as fiscal agents, and as promoting and being responsible for securities of the railroad system, under no sort of obligation to discourage or prevent a competing railroad?"

"No, sir."

"You know a competing railroad might ruin you?"

"I could not help that."

"You would not try to help it?"

"Something might occur that would necessitate it. I cannot say what I would do, but on general principles I should not."

Untermyer returned to the central issue of the hearings. "I want to ask you a few questions bearing on the subject that you have touched upon this morning, as to the control of money. The control of credit involves a control of money, does it not?"

"A control of credit? No."

"But the basis of banking is credit, is it not?"

"Not always. That is an evidence of banking, but it is not the money itself. Money is gold, and nothing else."

"Is there any country in the world of which the outstanding obligations passing as money are supported dollar for dollar by gold?"

"It comes nearer to it in England than anywhere else."

Untermyer asked again about credit. "A man or a group of men who have the control of credit have control of money, have they not?"

"No, sir, not always."

"That is generally so, is it not?"

"No."

"If you had the control of all that represents the assets in the banks of New York, you would have the control of all that money?"

"No, sir, not in my opinion. It may be wrong, but that is my opinion."

"Money is a commodity, and you know you can control any other commodity, do you not?"

"I do not think so," Morgan said. "You can control business, but you cannot control money."

"If a man controlled the credit of a country, he would have a control of all its affairs?"

"He might have that, but he would not have the money. If he had the credit and I had the money, his customer would be badly off." Morgan repeated: "Money cannot be controlled."

But didn't money make credit possible?

Morgan shook his head. "I know lots of men, business men, too, who can borrow any amount, whose credit is unquestioned."

"Is that not so because it is believed that they have the money back of them?"

"No, sir. It is because people believe in the man."

"And is regardless of whether he has any financial backing at all?"

"It is, very often."

"And he might not be worth anything?"

"He might not have anything. I have known men to come into my office, and I have given them a check for a million dollars when I knew they had not a cent in the world."

Untermyer evinced incredulity. "There are not many of them?"

"Yes, a good many," Morgan insisted.

"Is not commercial credit based primarily on money or property?"

"No, sir; the first thing is character."

"Before money or property?"

"Before money or anything else. Money cannot buy it."

"So that a man with character, without anything at all behind it, can get all the credit he wants, and a man with the property cannot get it?"

"That is very often the case."

"That is the rule of business?"

"That is the rule of business, sir."

Untermyer frowned. He asked Morgan to imagine a man walking into his bank. "If he has got government bonds or railroad bonds, and goes in to get credit, he gets it, and on the security of those bonds, does he not? He does not get it on his face or his character, does he?"

"He gets it on his character."

Untermyer interrupted. "Then he might as well take the bonds home?"

Morgan continued: "Because a man I do not trust could not get money from me for all the bonds in Christendom."

None knew it that December day, but Morgan's round with Untermyer marked his last public appearance. He sailed to Europe on his annual art-buying tour, fell ill aboard his yacht on the Nile, retreated to Rome and expired there. His friends blamed the inquisition before the Pujo panel, asserting that if Untermyer had treated him with the respect he deserved he would still be alive to serve the common weal.

Whatever the cause of death, Morgan's passing marked the eclipse of the financial system he had come to dominate. Andrew Carnegie marveled at Morgan's leverage. "And to think, he was not a rich man," Carnegie said on learning that Morgan's disposable estate totaled but $68 million and that only $30 million was in bank shares. Carnegie was many times wealthier than Morgan, and John Rockefeller was richer than Carnegie. But Morgan's reach exceeded Carnegie's or Rockefeller's; as the maestro of American money, he conducted the music to which the industrialists—and everyone else—danced.

Which was the point Pujo and the money-trust committee made against Morgan in the report they filed with Congress. The report detailed the interlocking directorates of American financial firms, starting with Morgan and spreading outward. Decrying the "great and rapidly growing concentration of the control of money and credit in the hands of these few men," the Pujo report concluded: "The peril is manifest."

Reducing the peril and offsetting the bankers' control of money fell improbably to Benjamin Strong. The Bankers' Trust chairman liked to recall a critical moment during the Morgan rescue of 1907 when he had personally delivered the down payment on a part of the package that sustained the beleaguered Trust Company of America. He got the money from National City Bank, which had funds to spare. "I remember giving Mr. Whitson a pencil receipt for a bundle of gold certificates," Strong recounted. "I cannot now recall whether it was $600,000 or $1,000,000, but I put them in my pocket, ran down Wall Street, and at almost exactly ten o'clock found Mr. Thorne [of the Trust Company] walking up and down the gallery overlooking the banking room in the utmost anxiety lest he be disappointed in the loan. The minute he saw me he said that the trust companies had failed him, the money was not forthcoming, and that he expected to close the institution promptly at ten. The look of relief on his face when I handed him the first earnest money I shall never forget."

After the panic subsided, Strong joined other bankers and some public officials in working to ensure that another such fright not occur. A secret meeting took place on the Georgia coast in 1910, organized by Morgan partner Henry Davison and Rhode Island senator Nelson Aldrich. Morgan and his friends used Jekyll Island as a hunting resort; the gathering was billed as a boys' weekend out. Aldrich emerged with the outline of a bill he would introduce to the Senate, a measure intended to bolster the dollar and stabilize the American financial system by creating a "National Reserve Association." The association would act as a central bank, coordinating the activities of member banks around the country, issuing notes that would serve as money, setting interest rates and providing backup in the event of local or regional crises. Reflecting the business interests of the Jekyll Island bankers and the conservative philosophy of the Republican Aldrich, the reserve association would be controlled and directed by America's leading bankers.

The Aldrich plan showed promise till the Pujo committee put Morgan on the witness stand and demonstrated the daunting power the big bankers already wielded over the economy. The progressives in Congress, more full of themselves than ever following the 1912 election of Woodrow Wilson, the Democratic governor of New Jersey, had no desire to give the bankers any more leverage. They set the Aldrich plan aside and backed a substitute named for Carter Glass of Virginia, which would place control of the reserve association in a board of directors appointed by the president.

Benjamin Strong denounced the Glass bill as "fatally defective." Its leadership provisions were wrongheaded and insulting. "Supervisory power vested in the reserve board should be exercised by bankers of great skill and experience, and not by a body of political appointees and government officials," he said. "This bill reflects a profound distrust of a large body of capable and honest businessmen, namely the officers and directors of the national banks." When a version of the Glass bill, modified by Senator Robert Owen of Oklahoma, gained traction in Congress during the autumn of 1913, Strong did his best to block it. "I believe every intelligent loyal citizen of this country should register the strongest possible protest and refuse to entertain a suggestion of compromise," he wrote a banking friend.

But Strong's protests, like those of other big bankers, came to naught. In December, Congress passed and Wilson signed the Federal Reserve Act. The measure authorized the establishment of a system of regional Federal Reserve banks, privately owned and directed, operating under the aegis of a Federal Reserve Board. The board would consist of the secretary of the treasury, the comptroller of the currency and five members appointed by the president with the advice and consent of the Senate. The board would oversee the activities of the regional banks and manage the Federal Reserve system.

The Fed board would also supervise the issuing of a new version of the dollar, embodied in Federal Reserve notes backed by both the federal government and by gold. "The said notes shall be obligations of the United States and shall be receivable by all national and member banks and Federal Reserve banks and for all taxes, customs, and other public dues," the law declared. "They shall be redeemed in gold on demand at the Treasury Department of the United States, in the city of Washington, District of Columbia, or in gold or lawful money at any Federal Reserve bank."

The Federal Reserve system heralded a new day in the history of the dollar and a new era—its sponsors hoped—in the balance between Wall Street and the rest of the country. "We have created a democracy of credit such as has never existed in this country before," Wilson exulted. "No group of bankers anywhere can get control; no one part of the country can concentrate the advantages and conveniences of the system upon itself for its own selfish advantage."

Benjamin Strong didn't disagree with Wilson, although he disliked the president's triumphal tone. Strong had opposed the bill and lost; now he prepared to move on. "We must all bend our energies in making the best of it," he wrote an ally-in-defeat. "I do not think it will be the part of wisdom to embarrass the government in its efforts to develop the plan."

Far from embarrassing the government, Strong took the government's part as implementer-in-chief of the new law. As the regional banks were established—twelve in number— no one doubted that the most important would be situated in New York City. And when the organizers of the New York bank approached Strong to be its director, or governor, he accepted. The Federal Reserve Board was a novelty; it would require time to find its way forward. But a Federal Reserve *bank* was, after all, a bank. Strong understood banks, and, as head of the most important Federal Reserve bank, he became the dynamo of the new system.

And this dynamo had a mind and will of his own. Strong had favored a strong central authority during the bill-crafting phase, but he now came to see merit in the dispersal of author-

33

ity. "The principles of a central bank (as distinguished from regional banks) I believe to be sound, thoroughly practicable in this country, and, in the long run, a much more economical and effective method of dealing with the reserve question," he remarked. But he worried that a central bank would be subject to outside pressure. Referring to Nicholas Biddle's defeat by Andrew Jackson, he explained: "I do not believe a central bank could be kept alive in the face of political attack today any more than it could in 1836." Strong never lost his fear of political influence distorting the purposes of the Fed, or seeming to. "I have been haunted, as you know, by the possibility of charges of misuse of the Federal Reserve System for political purposes," he wrote a friend years later. "Perhaps I am oversensitive on the subject. My attitude may be expressed by the case of the chap whose wife went abroad to take care of her sick mother. When he got a cable from his wife that his mother-in-law was dead, and asking whether she should bury, embalm, or cremate the remains, he replied, 'All three. Take no chances.' That is exactly my attitude on this and a few other matters relating to the System."

In the event it wasn't political attack that Strong had to worry about, but military attack. The establishment of the Federal Reserve system coincided with the outbreak of war in Europe, which swiftly overturned nearly everything Strong and most other bankers had come to expect of the world of finance. The first effect of the war was to drain gold from American vaults as the British, French and Germans called in their American loans and demanded gold in payment. Exports of the yellow metal hit record highs, raising the specter once again that the dollar would have to be severed from gold. But the tide soon shifted. Neutral countries looked to American producers for goods they had previously purchased from the belligerents, and then Britain, France and to a much lesser degree Germany began increasing their purchases of American products. Gold flowed back into the United States, filling American vaults to the ceiling. And when the belligerents ran out of gold, they borrowed dollars. The United States, a heavy net debtor at the beginning of the war, became the world's largest creditor by the war's end. The dollar, under dire threat during the war's first months, became the world's leading currency.

The war also effected a revolution in American federal finance, with the help of the sixteenth amendment to the constitution. From the founding of the republic through the end of the nineteenth century, the operations of the federal government had been funded primarily through the sale of public lands and the collection of tariffs on imports. Congress passed an income tax law during the Civil War, but this was subsequently voided by the Supreme Court as violating the constitution's ban on direct taxes not apportioned according to the populations of the states. The sixteenth amendment, ratified in early 1913, explicitly allowed unapportioned income taxes.

The first tax rates were very modest, topping out at 2 percent on incomes over $20,000. But when the United States began arming for war, and then when the country joined the war, the need to expand government revenues forced a drastic upward revision of the rates, to a maximum of 77 percent on incomes over a million dollars. Combined with a reduction in tariff revenues, as a result of the war's disruption of imports and a revision of the tariff schedules, the increase in the tax rates by the war's end shifted the burden of federal finance dramatically in the direction of the income tax (where it has remained ever since).

But the taxes didn't cover the whole cost of the war. The government sold bonds, nearly $25 billion worth. An unconsidered consequence of this debt was to permit the Federal Reserve to engage in open-market operations. The Fed could purchase bonds from banks, paying in dollars that increased the banks' reserves and allowed the banks to expand their loans. Or it could sell bonds to banks, reducing the banks' reserves and compelling a reduction of loans. This process permitted a calibration of the money supply beyond the original conception of the Fed's powers and beyond what would have been possible in the absence of such a large circulation of government bonds.

The Fed's new tool was put to the test in the wake of the war. High demand for American commodities produced severe inflation; Fed officials sought to wrestle prices back down. "The day of deflation approaches," Strong wrote in early 1919. It wouldn't be pleasant when it came. "The process of deflation is a painful one, involving loss, unemployment, bankruptcy and social and political disorders."

Yet the pain wouldn't be America's alone, or even America's mostly. The war left the British and French in hock to the United States, and the Germans, as a result of the draconian Versailles treaty, in financial bondage to the British and French. Many observers deemed the peace settlement a formula for another war; John Maynard Keynes, an emerging economist who served with the British delegation at Paris, stormed out of the conference to denounce the whole charade. The reparations imposed on Germany were impossibly punitive, Keynes said. "Germany has in effect engaged herself to hand over to the Allies the whole of her surplus production." The payment schedule "skins her alive year by year in perpetuity, and however skillfully and discreetly the operation is performed, with whatever regard for not killing the patient in the process, it would represent a policy which, if it were really entertained and deliberately practiced, the judgment of men would soon pronounce to be one of the most outrageous acts of a cruel victor in civilized history."

Keynes decried the financial implications of the treaty. "Lenin is said to have declared that the best way to destroy the capitalist system was to debauch the currency"; the treaty guaranteed that Germany would do its best to debauch the capitalist world's currencies, to ease its reparations burden. The inflation that would result would act most insidiously. "The process engages all the hidden forces of economic law on the side of destruction, and does it in a manner which not one man in a million is able to diagnose." Most ominously, the strangling of Germany economically would have political consequences. "Economic privation proceeds by easy stages, and so long as men suffer it patiently the outside world cares little. Physical efficiency and resistance to disease slowly diminish, but life proceeds somehow, until the limit of human endurance is reached at last and counsels of despair and madness stir the sufferers from the lethargy which precedes the crisis. Then man shakes himself, and the bonds of custom are loosed. The power of ideas is sovereign, and he listens to whatever instruction of hope, illusion, or revenge is carried to him on the air." Keynes wrote with an eye to mitigating the severity of the peace, but he feared he was too late. "If this view of nations and of their relation to one another is adopted by the democracies of Western Europe, and is financed by the United States, heaven help us all."

Benjamin Strong shared Keynes's concern about the future of Europe, but one part of Keynes's brief gave him particular pause. "The existence of the great war debts is a menace to financial stability everywhere," Keynes wrote. "Entangling alliances or entangling leagues are nothing to the entanglements of cash owing." Strong appreciated how the war and specifically the war's funding had transformed America's financial position, and he understood that Europe's troubles were America's troubles, regardless of what the politicians decided. When the politicians—the Senate specifically—rejected the Versailles treaty and Americans at large tried to turn their backs on Europe, Strong buckled down to what he realized would be a thankless task.

He traveled to London to assess things on the ground. "The immediate task now ahead of us, which will help conditions over here more than anything else, is to get some sort of a definition of the terms of the debt of the Allies to the United States, and particularly of the British debt," he wrote home. The Brit-

ish and French were touchy. "There is undoubtedly in existence here a latent underlying feeling that the Allies have made
the great and most vital sacrifices in the war, both of men and
finance and in material damage suffered; that our sacrifices
have been slight and our profits immense, and that the existence of this great debt due on demand is a sword of Damocles
hanging over their heads." Strong didn't care much about the
French, who mattered modestly in world finance, but he valued the good opinion of the British, the keepers of the key to
Europe's financial future—and America's, he judged. "England
and the United States must in some way preserve good relations and work together."

What they worked on most assiduously was returning the
world to the gold standard. The war had driven Britain and
most other belligerents off gold; at war's end only the United
States, of the world's big economic powers, still attached its
currency to gold. Benjamin Strong and his counterparts in
Britain, especially Montagu Norman, the head of the Bank of
England, considered the revival of the international gold standard crucial to economic stability and growth and the avoid-
ance of future wars. Both men had additional reasons peculiar
to their own countries. For Norman the gold standard was a
source of Britain's legitimacy as a global power. Britain had led
the world to gold during the nineteenth century; if it wanted to
lead the world to anything in the twentieth century, gold would
play a large part. For Strong the return of Britain—and other
countries—to gold seemed necessary in order to bleed inflation from the American economy. Gold continued to pour into
the United States; as banks issued loans against this gold, the
American money supply expanded and created upward pressure on prices. "We now hold one-half of the world's monetary
gold, and our holdings increase steadily," Strong observed to
Andrew Mellon, the treasury secretary, in 1924. "Our own
interests demand that no effort be spared to secure a return to
the gold standard, and so arrest the flood of gold which threat-
ens in time to plunge us into inflation."

Strong could discourage inflows of gold by employing the tools of the Fed to reduce interest rates. As the return on government bonds and other instruments fell, international gold looked for other employment, especially in Britain, where Montagu Norman kept British interest rates high. The joint thinking of Strong and Norman was that once Britain's gold reserves returned to something like their prewar level, Britain could safely readopt the gold standard.

The problem with this approach was that the low interest rates in America encouraged investments that might not have been made otherwise and perhaps *should* not have been made. "We have had a dangerous speculation develop in the stock market, with some evidence that it is extending into commodities," Strong wrote Norman in the autumn of 1925. "There has been a rampaging real estate speculation in some spots." The responsibility of the Fed for averting or puncturing bubbles in corporate shares and real estate would provoke debate for decades; in the early days of the Fed's existence Strong contended that the Fed ought to counter such bubbles.

But he wasn't sure how to do it. The New York Fed could raise interest rates, and the increase would certainly dampen speculation, but the effect would probably wear off over time. "The bad news would be out, and, after a severe shock to the stock market, it would go off on its merry way again," he wrote Norman. The prospect of rate increases might be more effective in cooling speculation than the actuality. "We could better control it as a psychological problem by keeping a sword of Damocles suspended over the speculator."

There was no easy answer. "Every situation like the present one is a puzzle," Strong wrote as the economy roared forward. "There seem to be three developments which have the possibility of harm. One is overbuilding and real estate speculation. Another is too much enthusiasm in automobile production, and the third, of course, is the ever-present menace of the stock exchange speculation." He didn't know how much of a response he and the Fed ought to make. "Must we accept parenthood for every economic development in the country? That is a hard thing for us to do. We would have a large family of children. Every time any one of them misbehaved, we might have to spank them all. There is no selective process in credit operations. . . . Have we infallible good judgment as well as sufficient knowledge to play the role of parent, and attempt to restrain every unwholesome boom, and as a concomitant undertake to correct every class of business which shows signs of languishing? May it not be the case that the world is now entering upon a period where business developments will follow the recovery of confidence, so long lost as a result of the war? Nobody knows, and I will not dare to prophesy."

Strong kept interest rates low long enough to usher the British back onto the gold standard. The strengthening pound helped the dollar stabilize the global economy. The dollar needed all the help it could get, for Europe was suffering many of the ills John Maynard Keynes had forecast. The Germans attempted to inflate their way out of their reparations corner, until the mark lost all semblance of value. Shivering German families burned the mark notes for fuel, so plentiful and worthless had they become. The United States government participated in a partial resolution of the debt problem by sending banker Charles Dawes to Europe to negotiate a reduction in German reparations and an increase in lending—mostly by American banks—to Germany. The Dawes plan closed the circle of payments: American dollars enabled the Germans to pay reparations to the British and French, who used the reparations to repay the debts they owed the Americans. The entire process bolstered the dollar's position as the fundamental currency of international finance.

Strong nonetheless worried that the positive trends wouldn't last. The Republicans, long the party of high tariffs, were up to their protectionist mischief again. A proposed new tariff schedule was particularly pernicious, Strong told a friend, who happened to be a Republican bigwig, "This bill proceeds upon the essentially unsound and vicious doctrine that a nation can grow rich out of its export trade. Nothing could be more fallacious, especially in the case of a nation which has a wealth of raw materials for export. Nations grow rich out of *trade*, out of the *exchange* of commodities which it produces by reason of special resources or special talents to better advantage than other nations, and they are paid for those goods by importing goods produced under like advantages by other nations. . . . If we expect to get the debts owing us by Europe paid, we must import more than we export. If we put a prohibitive tariff upon imports, we by so much restrict our exports, and further make it impossible for those who owe us money to pay it."

He worried as well that the necessary end to the easy-money policies that had brought Britain back onto gold would alarm the speculators who had grown used to the low rates. "The problem now is so to shape our policy as to avoid a calamitous break in the stock market," he wrote in the summer of 1928. The transition would be tricky but not impossible. "I certainly think it can be done."

And if Wall Street took fright at higher interest rates, the Fed could step in. "The very existence of the Federal Reserve System is a safeguard against anything like a calamity growing out of money rates," Strong said. "Not only have we the power to deal with such an emergency instantly by flooding the street with money, but I think the country is well aware of this and probably places reliance upon the common sense and power of the System. In former days the psychology was different because the facts of the banking situation were different. Mob panic, and consequently mob disaster, is less likely to arise."

≡ SKULLS AND BONES ≡

1929–1944

Benjamin Strong had suffered from tuberculosis for more than a decade. The respiratory ailment took him away from his work for increasing periods, and complications of the disease finally carried him off in October 1928, at the age of fifty-five.

Had he lived, he might have summoned the nerve to follow his own advice about "flooding the street with money" amid the stock market crash of October 1929. The crash caught investors by rude surprise, although more as to timing than to the fact of a fall. Market boosters had hailed a "new era" in American finance, saying that such modern techniques and technologies as the assembly line and electricity had forever changed American business and hence the American stock market, but seasoned observers reflected that every bull market had eventually ended, and they assumed this one would, too. Joseph Kennedy, one of the shrewdest speculators on Wall Street, pulled back after receiving unsolicited investment advice from his shoeshine man. Bernard Baruch, another market pro, warned a tip-seeking novice to clear out. "You're sitting on a volcano," Baruch said. "That's all right for professional volcano sitters like myself, but an amateur like you ought to take to the tall timber and get as far away as you can."

When the volcano erupted, it rocked American finance to the foundations. Banks had long dabbled in the stock market, but during the 1920s the dabbling became a primary enterprise. The rapid rise in stock prices tempted bankers to put their depositors' money in Wall Street shares rather than Main Street mortgages; till October 1929 those many bankers who succumbed to the temptation looked like geniuses. But once stocks collapsed, the bankers discovered they couldn't cover their deposits, and the falling stock shares knocked over the banks in daunting numbers.

The banks, in turn, took down much of the rest of the economy. Individual customers lost their deposits, in the process losing much of their purchasing power. The bank failures caused credit markets to seize up; even businesses and individuals far removed from the carnage in the stock market and the failure of the banks discovered that they weren't so distant after all. Businesses couldn't borrow to finance inventory and payrolls; farmers couldn't borrow to buy seeds and fertilizer; consumers couldn't borrow to buy houses or autos. The concept of a death spiral was comparatively new, as aviation remained a novelty in much of the country, but as a metaphor describing the state of the economy it seemed soberingly apt. Each evil influence amplified the others: declining stocks weakened the banks and tightened credit, which damaged companies' profitability and caused stocks to fall further; worker layoffs reduced buying power, battering profits the more, which prompted employers to lay off additional workers. The economy's descent grew steeper and steeper.

A firm hand and a bold heart at the Fed might have pulled the economy out of its dive. A flood of credit could have kept businesses open, farmers in the field, workers on the job. But the requisite leadership didn't exist. Benjamin Strong was dead and no one stepped forward to take his place. Rather than stem the panic and avert the depression that followed, the Fed contributed to the debacle. It not only failed to make credit available but allowed the money supply to shrink an asphyxiating 30 percent between 1929 and 1933. Strong's successors believed the contraction a necessary corrective to the speculation that had gone before. "The present crisis through which we are passing is typical of the kind of crisis the framers of the Federal Reserve Act had in mind," Fed member Charles S. Hamlin asserted. "The Federal Reserve System was designed to break up the vicious circle under which a speculative orgy accompanied every forward step of industry. . . . These events are deplorable, but they were of course inevitable and could not have been avoided."

The Fed wasn't alone in aggravating the crisis. Congress indulged the protectionist tendencies Strong had warned against. Republican congressman Willis Hawley of Oregon joined Republican senator Reed Smoot of Utah in sponsoring a tariff bill that raised duties on a broad range of imports. Congress approved the bill and sent it to President Hoover. Wall Street tried to intervene. "I almost went down on my knees to beg Herbert Hoover to veto the asinine Hawley-Smoot tariff," Thomas Lamont of J. P. Morgan & Company explained afterward. A thousand economists from all over the country petitioned Hoover to reject the new protectionism. "Increased restrictive duties would be a mistake," the economists declared. "They would operate, in general, to increase the prices which domestic consumers would have to pay." The duties would subsidize inefficiency in the protected industries while harming unprotected producers. "Miners, construction, transportation and public utility workers, professional people and those employed in banks, hotels, newspaper offices, in the wholesale and retail trades and scores of other occupations would clearly lose, since they produce no products which would be specially favored by tariff barriers." Exports would fall as other countries retaliated, dealing a punishing blow to the world economy and poisoning the atmosphere of international relations. "A tariff war does not furnish good soil for the growth of world peace."

Hoover signed the bill anyway. And the consequences the

economists predicted came true. Canada, America's largest trading partner, retaliated at once; other countries joined the protectionist parade. International exports languished. International bitterness grew.

By the summer of 1932 America was plumbing the depths of the worst depression in its history. A quarter of the workforce was unemployed; production had fallen by a third; the stock market had lost four-fifths of its value. Hoover devised various schemes for dealing with the crisis; one or more might have worked, given time. But with the depression in its third year and Hoover's presidency in its fourth, Americans weren't willing to give him more time. Their impression of the president was of someone out of touch, even callous—an impression that was intensified amid the most dramatic event of the summer, a gathering of military veterans from the world war who wanted Congress to prepay a pension scheduled for 1945. The vets were a mostly miserable bunch: jobless, homeless and, if Congress denied their petition, hopeless. Only to the fevered imagination of Hoover—and the Napoleonic imagination of his army chief of staff, Douglas MacArthur—did the ragtag "bonus army" appear ominous. But Hoover ordered the army to disperse the vets, and MacArthur carried out the order with a vengeance. His tanks and machine-gunners rolled through the camp where the vets had gathered with their wives and children. Scores were injured; one child was killed. The bloody affair convinced millions of Americans that Hoover was fatally out of touch with the plight of common folk.

"Well, Felix, this will elect me," Franklin Roosevelt told Felix Frankfurter regarding the rout of the veterans. Roosevelt was governor of New York and the Democrats' candidate to replace Hoover. His background had prepared him more fully to be president than almost any candidate before him (or after); ever since his fifth cousin Theodore Roosevelt had assumed the presidency, while Franklin was in college, the younger man had reckoned how he might follow the elder's footsteps. He visited Theodore in the White House, measured himself against the Rough Rider and decided that what Theodore had done, he could do as well. He tightened the connection by marrying Theodore's niece Eleanor Roosevelt. At the wedding of Franklin and Eleanor, Theodore congratulated the groom and laughingly declared, "There's nothing like keeping the name in the family!"

Franklin Roosevelt pursued Theodore's script in twice winning election to the New York state legislature. He mimicked TR in taking the post of assistant navy secretary in Washington. In Franklin's case the job became more than the stepping-stone it had been for Theodore; after Europe went to war in 1914 and the United States followed in 1917, the navy post proved one of the most crucial in Washington. Franklin Roosevelt watched Wilson lead the country into the war and then out of the war, with the ungainly exit—via the Senate's rejection of the Versailles treaty—frustrating Wilson's hopes for a continuing American role in securing the peace and the stability of the world. Roosevelt, appreciating the strength of American isolationist sentiment, determined not to repeat Wilson's mistakes.

His path to the White House took a detour in 1921 when he contracted polio. The illness paralyzed his legs and carried him out of politics—at a time when being out of politics served a useful career purpose. The economic boom of the 1920s rendered Republicans nearly invulnerable; Roosevelt recognized their strength and made no hurry to get back into the game. He eventually accepted a draft for the Democratic nomination for New York governor in 1928 and won a close contest, thereby returning to the Theodore Roosevelt route. When the stock market crashed the next year and the broader economy followed it down, the Democratic governor of the nation's most populous state seemed an obvious alternative to the discredited Hoover. The bonus army fiasco sealed the deal.

Yet Hoover didn't leave quietly. He lost the election badly but spent the five-month interregnum intriguing to commit

Roosevelt to maintaining the dollar's value against gold. Roosevelt hadn't thought deeply about monetary policy; governors, even the governor of the state that encompasses Wall Street, don't make decisions about the value, quantity and convertibility of money. But Roosevelt vaguely believed the dollar was overvalued. Prices had been falling for years for agricultural products, and the depression had exacerbated the problems this caused indebted farmers. Roosevelt hadn't decided what he was going to do about the situation, but he didn't want Hoover to tie his hands before he even entered office.

Hoover had more in mind than defending the dollar. "I realize that if these declarations are made by the President-elect, he will have ratified the whole major program of the Republican administration," Hoover told an associate. "That is, it means the abandonment of 90 percent of the so-called new deal." He thought this necessary for the good of the country. "Unless this is done, they run a grave danger of precipitating a complete financial debacle."

Hoover's maneuvering, combined with Roosevelt's refusal to be drawn in, made the bad situation worse. Observers—reporters, investors and the general public—naturally interpreted Roosevelt's refusal to endorse Hoover's affirmation of the gold dollar at current rates as indicating at least the possibility he would devalue the dollar, or perhaps detach it from gold entirely. Gold poured out of the country by the hundreds of millions of dollars; dollars poured out of America's banks as depositors feared for the banks' liquidity. Additional hundreds, then thousands, of banks buckled under the strain. Governors of several states declared "bank holidays"—a euphemism borrowed from Britain to indicate government-ordered suspensions of bank operations. The holidays didn't solve the problem and may have exacerbated it by closing sound banks along with the unsound and casting the shadow of doubt over all of them. But the measures postponed the day of reckoning, at least until Roosevelt's inauguration.

"The only thing we have to fear is fear itself: nameless, unreasoning, unjustified terror which paralyzes needed efforts to convert retreat into advance," Roosevelt told the country in his inaugural address. He proceeded contradictorily to itemize the all-too-real reasons for fear. "Values have shrunken to fantastic levels; taxes have risen; our ability to pay has fallen; government of all kinds is faced by serious curtailment of income; the means of exchange are frozen in the currents of trade; the withered leaves of industrial enterprise lie on every side; farmers find no markets for their produce; the savings of many years in thousands of families are gone. More important, a host of unemployed citizens face the grim problem of existence, and an equally great number toil with little return. Only a foolish optimist can deny the dark realities of the moment."

Roosevelt blamed Wall Street for America's dire condition. "Rulers of the exchange of mankind's goods have failed through their own stubbornness and their own incompetence. . . . They know only the rules of a generation of self-seekers. They have no vision, and when there is no vision the people perish." Fortunately, change was at hand. "The money changers have fled from their high seats in the temple of our civilization. We may now restore that temple to the ancient truths. The measure of the restoration lies in the extent to which we apply social values more noble than mere monetary profit. Happiness lies not in the mere possession of money; it lies in the joy of achievement, in the thrill of creative effort." The American people had spoken. "This nation asks for action, and action now!"

The new president gave the nation what he said it wanted. He summoned a special session of Congress and extended the state-by-state bank holidays to the entire country. To alleviate pressure on the dollar, he specifically forbade "the withdrawal or transfer in any manner or by any device whatsoever, of any gold or silver coin or bullion or currency."

No president had ever taken such bold action with respect to the dollar. Roosevelt wasn't even sure it was legal. He cited a provision of the 1917 Trading with the Enemy Act, which had never been repealed. But credible legal opinion held that such wartime legislation lapsed automatically on the end of the war. Roosevelt solicited a second opinion, from his attorney-general-designate, who declared the law still in effect.

Legality aside, Roosevelt knew he was taking a huge risk. By freezing the nation's assets he bought himself time to fix the problems that underlay the financial crisis. But he had only days: the country couldn't live without banks—which was to say, without ready cash—for long. The economy, already struggling, would soon clank to a halt.

He threw the pertinent members of his administration into discussions with the leaders of Congress on the shape of a rescue package for the banks. The weakest banks would be closed; the less damaged would be taken over by the stronger banks. The president would set a timetable for reopening the banks. Government money—in the form of loans from the Federal Reserve to banks, and of new Federal Reserve notes that would augment the money supply—would bolster the whole system.

Congress passed the Emergency Banking Act without most members having read it. The bill hadn't returned from the printer when the House conducted its vote; the representatives passed judgment on a crumpled newspaper that served as proxy for the measure.

Roosevelt signed the act on Thursday evening, March 9. Three days later, on Sunday night, he commandeered the nation's airwaves to deliver the first of what came to be known as "fireside chats." Winter still gripped most of the country; in millions of households people had already crawled into bed to conserve fuel. They heard Roosevelt the way children hear their fathers bid them good night as they tuck them in. The president didn't speak long—less than fifteen minutes. But in that brief time he talked to the country more directly about money and finance than any president had before. He explained how the banking business worked and how it had lately failed to work. He told what he and the Congress had done by way of the banking act to fix the failure and put things right. He laid out the schedule on which the banks would reopen, starting the next morning. And he delineated the crucial role of the American people in making the new system work. "After all, there is an element in the readjustment of our financial system more important than currency, more important than gold," he said. "And that is the confidence of the people. Confidence and courage are the essentials of success in carrying out our plan. You people must have faith; you must not be stampeded by rumors or guesses. Let us unite in banishing fear. We have provided the machinery to restore our financial system; it is up to you to support and make it work. It is your problem no less than it is mine. Together we cannot fail."

Roosevelt's appeal effected a magical transformation in the mood of the country. During the next three days, as the banks reopened, depositors once more lined up outside the doors. But where for months they had been taking money *out* of the banks, now they began putting money back *in*. This popular vote of confidence buoyed the stock market, which registered its biggest gains in years. Within two weeks most of the money that had been withdrawn from the banks returned; by the middle of the following month the banking crisis had passed.

The dollar crisis remained, however. The rescue of the banks, which eased the pressure on the dollar, in one important respect made America's economic situation worse. The depression had hit other industrial countries harder than it hit the United States; less robust to begin with, they suffered more. Their currencies reflected their pain. The British were forced off the gold standard in 1931; the Germans and various other European countries similarly severed their currencies from gold. The continued attachment of the dollar to gold made American products expensive in foreign markets, intensifying the damage the tariff wars were doing to American exports.

Reporters at Roosevelt's first press conference asked him about his policy on the dollar and gold. Would he follow London and take America off the gold standard?

Roosevelt responded cryptically. "Nobody knows what the

gold basis or gold standard really is," he said. "If you want a definition of the gold standard, read my friend Robey's story in the *New York Evening Post*." Ralph Robey was an economist and occasional consultant to the administration. Roosevelt paraphrased Robey to the reporters. Robey—and Roosevelt—identified four characteristics of a meaningful gold standard. The first was that the gold value of the currency must be clearly articulated. "Well, of course on that first requisite we are on the gold standard," Roosevelt said, referring to the statutory exchange rate of $20.67 per ounce. The second characteristic was free and unlimited coinage of gold. Whatever amount of gold was delivered to the government must be minted into coins or used to support dollar notes. "We are still on the gold standard," Roosevelt said of this second trait. "And the more people who bring gold to have it made into money the better." The third property was the ready redemption of paper notes into gold. The United States had various forms of paper money, but under the Gold Standard Act of 1900, still in force, all were required to be kept at par with gold. "Well, you can draw your own conclusions about that," Roosevelt said. Before the reporters could ask what conclusions *he* would draw, he proceeded to the fourth characteristic of a gold standard: the free movement of gold into and out of the country professing the gold standard. "For a good long time, as a matter of actual fact, the United States has been the only country on the gold standard," Roosevelt said. "France has been theoretically on a gold standard, but nobody in France can take a bill to the bank and get gold for it; and, as far as imports and exports go in France, they have been government-controlled." In the United States: "Up to last Sunday night"—the night of his bank-closing order—"we have had free trade in gold; and now we haven't."

The reporters asked whether the administration would return to free trade in gold. Roosevelt wouldn't say. One reporter quoted the president's inaugural address, in which he called for a "sound and adequate" currency.

"I put it the other way around," Roosevelt corrected. "I said 'adequate but sound.'"

"Can you define what that is?"

"No." Amid the nervous laughter that followed, Roosevelt added, "In other words—and I should call this off-the-record information—you cannot define the thing too closely one way or the other."

Roosevelt kept reporters and everyone else guessing until the summer of 1933, when delegates from nearly all the countries of the world gathered in London for a conference on the international monetary system. The organizers of the conference viewed the depression as global in nature and therefore requiring global solutions. They looked to the United States, the country possessing the world's most powerful economy and the most important currency, to take the lead in devising those solutions.

Roosevelt was reluctant. Though an internationalist at heart—he had been a strong supporter of the League of Nations and remained quietly convinced that America should be involved in international efforts to ensure peace and stability—he recognized the strength of American isolationism. Americans had long looked askance at the motives of other governments, and for Roosevelt to be seen as carrying water for those other governments would be damaging politically. More to the financial point, Roosevelt believed that the solution to America's depression must begin with a devaluation of the dollar. In no other way could he envision getting domestic prices back up to where farmers and other struggling producers would have a reasonable chance of prosperity.

Roosevelt nonetheless played along with the conference awhile. He let Cordell Hull, his secretary of state, deliver an address on the need for international cooperation. "If we are to succeed, narrow and self-defeating selfishness must be banished from every human heart within this council chamber," Hull told the delegates. "If, which God forbid, any nation should obstruct and wreck this great conference with the short-sighted notion that some of its favored interests might temporarily profit while thus indefinitely delaying aid for the distressed in every country, that nation will merit the execration of mankind."

"I felt almost physically ill," Raymond Moley recalled of Hull's address. Moley was Hull's deputy by official posting but Roosevelt's secret agent on the side. Moley knew that Roosevelt intended no such altruism as Hull summoned, yet he didn't know why Roosevelt, who had read Hull's remarks in advance, allowed the secretary to raise the hopes of the conference.

The hopes were indeed raised, only to be dashed. The British and French wanted Roosevelt to agree to a system of fixed exchange rates. Such a system, they contended, was essential to economic recovery. Only when merchants and investors knew what each currency was worth relative to the others would they regain the confidence they required to get back about their business. Roosevelt refused to go along. He didn't think fixed rates were sustainable given the disarray of the world economy. Moreover, in tying the dollar to the pound and the franc he would be tying himself to British and French policy, limiting his ability to deal with the depression in America. Roosevelt wasn't as parochial as the isolationists, but he never forgot that he had been elected president of the United States and not ruler of the world. Each nation must find its own path out of the depression.

In July 1933 Roosevelt announced his refusal to cooperate with the conference. "The world will not long be lulled by the specious fallacy of achieving a temporary and probably an artificial stability in foreign exchange," he asserted from Washington. "The sound internal economic system of a nation is a greater factor in its well-being than the price of its currency in changing terms of the currencies of other nations." Speaking more prospectively and somewhat more positively, the president continued: "The United States seeks the kind of dollar which a generation hence will have the same purchasing and debt-paying power as the dollar value we hope to attain in the near future. That objective means more to the good of other nations than a fixed ratio for a month or two in terms of the pound or franc."

Roosevelt's announcement stunned the conference. The British were appalled. "America is the bonfire boy of the world," the London *Daily Express* declared. "She lights a fire which might have been a beacon, then runs away to watch it burn itself out." Prime Minister Ramsay MacDonald had staked his political future on cooperation with Roosevelt, whom he had visited in Washington ahead of the conference. "I have rarely seen a man more distraught than he was that morning," Ray Moley recalled of a postannouncement interview at 10 Downing Street. "He turned a grief-stricken face to me as I came in, and he cried out, 'This doesn't sound like the man I spent so many hours with in Washington. This sounds like a different man. I don't understand.'"

Roosevelt gradually made MacDonald, and the world, understand. Step by step he reengineered the value of the dollar. He directed the treasury to bid up the price of gold. Every morning he met with Henry Morgenthau, a close adviser who would become his treasury secretary; George Warren, a Cornell University professor who specialized in farm economics; and Jesse Jones, the director of the federal Reconstruction Finance Corporation, to discuss that day's gold purchases. Roosevelt, sitting in bed eating his soft-boiled eggs, would pick a number to serve as the target rise in the gold price. One morning Morgenthau, as frowningly serious as usual, suggested that something between 19 and 22 cents would be appropriate. Roosevelt immediately decided on 21 cents. "It's a lucky number, because it's three times seven," he said, laughing. Morgenthau considered the president's answer entirely too flippant. "If anybody ever knew how we really set the gold price, through a combination of lucky numbers, etc., I think they would really be frightened," Morgenthau recorded in his diary.

There was method to Roosevelt's gold-buying scheme, but not enough to please all the economists. George Warren contended that plumping gold would pull up farm prices. "A rise in prices is essential," Warren told Roosevelt. "The only way in which a rise in price can be brought about and held is by reducing the gold value of the dollar. . . . If the treasury is ordered to buy a certain amount of new gold at a certain price, and if the price is raised at frequent intervals, this would probably accomplish the purpose." Other economists vehemently rejected this argument. John Maynard Keynes blasted Warren's theories, and Roosevelt's policies, in an open letter in the *New York Times*. Keynes endorsed the concept of managing the value of the dollar, but he thought the president was going about it all wrong. "The recent gyrations of the dollar have looked to me more like a gold standard on the booze than the ideal managed currency of my dreams," Keynes said.

Yet Roosevelt's gold policy was less about economic theory than about political practice. The depression had inspired farmers' advocates to do what their predecessors during the last long depression, of the late nineteenth century, had done: insist on expansion of the currency as a way of raising prices. Senator Elmer Thomas of Oklahoma succeeded in attaching to the Agricultural Adjustment Act an amendment calling on the president to create new dollars by purchasing and monetizing silver, by issuing greenbacks or by altering the gold content of the dollar. Thomas had wanted to *require* the president to take such inflationary action; Roosevelt talked Thomas into letting the actions be discretionary. But the president felt the prairie wind that was rising behind Thomas, and he recognized the political perils in failing to exercise his discretion within the amendment's spirit. "Congratulate me," Roosevelt said with a wry smile to gathered aides as he indicated his acceptance of the Thomas amendment. "We are off the gold standard." Budget director Lewis Douglas didn't think congratulation was at all in order. "This is the end of Western civilization," he muttered.

The Thomas amendment encouraged the inflationists to

press for more. Congress approved a measure abrogating the gold clause that had been written into contracts since the days of the Civil War greenbacks, specifying payment in gold rather than paper currency. The abrogation was of dubious constitutionality, but it was popular with debtors. And it was anathema to creditors and their spokesmen. "It is simply incredible," Winthrop Aldrich, New York banker and son of Nelson Aldrich, said. Financier Bernard Baruch complained: "We're raising prices for the benefit of a small proportion—twenty percent— of the population, the unemployed, debtors classes—incompetent, unwise people." The abrogation foreshadowed grim days, Baruch said. "It can't be defended except as mob rule. Maybe the country doesn't know it yet, but I think we may find that we've been in a revolution more drastic than the French Revolution. The crowd has seized the seat of government and is trying to seize the wealth."

Roosevelt's gold-buying program split the difference between the determined inflationists and the defenders of the *ancien régime*. "What a task you have in your war against hunger and unemployment!" Russell Leffingwell, a rare sympathetic banker, wrote Roosevelt. "Between the deflationists who are sadists or radicals and want deflation to bring on revolution; the deflationists who are reactionaries, like Baruch; . . . and the extreme inflationists, like Father Coughlin [a populist radio personality], who can't know that that too means starvation and revolution. . . . Well, you are the captain, and you have always managed somehow. No doubt you will continue to do so, and to find some middle road between these extremes."

Roosevelt explained his middle road in a fireside chat in October 1933. "Ever since last March the definite policy of the government has been to restore commodity price levels," he said. "The object has been the attainment of such a level as will enable agriculture and industry once more to give work to the unemployed. It has been to make possible the payment of public and private debts more nearly at the price level at which they were incurred." Of course some people benefited from low prices and wanted the government to keep its hands off. This was what had led to the depression, Roosevelt said. Others wanted him to move faster: to devalue the dollar at once. This wouldn't do either. "It is the government's policy to restore the price level first. I would not know, and no one else could tell, just what the permanent valuation of the dollar will be. To guess at a permanent gold valuation now would certainly require later changes caused by later facts." The guiding intent of the administration was to restore prices to a fair level and to keep in American hands the control over the dollar. "Our dollar is now altogether too greatly influenced by the accidents of international trade, by the internal policies of other nations and by political disturbance in other continents. . . . The United States must take firmly in its own hands the control of the gold value of our dollar." The decision to purchase gold was an aspect of this program. "My aim in taking this step is to establish and maintain continuous control. This is a policy and not an expedient. It is not to be used merely to offset a temporary fall in prices." Doomsayers had criticized the policy from the start and hadn't stopped. "Prophets of evil still exist in our midst." But the policy would go forward. "Government credit will be maintained and a sound currency will accompany a rise in the American commodity price level."

Roosevelt followed his middle road to a gold price of $34 per ounce in late 1933. Then, in January 1934, Congress approved and the president signed the Gold Reserve Act, making his new policy permanent. The act fixed the price of gold—which was to say, fixed the value of the dollar—at $35 per ounce. This represented a nearly 60 percent devaluation from the long-standing conversion rate of $20.67 per ounce. In the bargain, the act required that Americans relinquish gold coin and bullion to the treasury, which stored it in Fort Knox.

The result was an odd compromise for the dollar, which remained linked to gold for foreigners but not for Americans. Traditionalists and even many populists wondered what theory underpinned Roosevelt's policy. He declined to inform them. Ray Moley concluded that instinct, not theory, was the key to understanding the president's policy. Moley was already having doubts regarding Roosevelt's grasp of the dismal science of economics, but he couldn't gainsay his understanding of the cheerful art of politics. "He was like the fairy-story prince who didn't know how to shudder," Moley reflected. "Not even the realization that he was playing nine-pins with the skulls and thighbones of economic orthodoxy seemed to worry him."

What *did* worry him, though, the more as time went on, was the threat to America and to democracy from the fascist regimes abroad. Democracy had failed in the 1920s in Italy, where Benito Mussolini's Fascists seized control; it was failing in Germany, where Adolf Hitler and the Nazis were crushing dissent; it was about to fail in Spain, where Francisco Franco and the Falange would overthrow the Spanish republic. Democracy had never taken root in Japan, but that country too was moving in an alarmingly authoritarian direction, and like Germany it was endangering the peace and security of its neighbors. After a first term devoted to domestic recovery— which came with agonizing slowness, and then retreated in a stinging recession in 1937—Roosevelt turned to foreign affairs in his second. In the autumn of 1937 he proposed to "quarantine" the aggression that had become a dismaying staple of international life. His suggestion failed to elicit the positive response he hoped for, and he confined himself to discreet diplomacy while awaiting a more likely opportunity.

The German invasion of Poland in September 1939, which prompted war declarations by Britain and France, gave Roosevelt the opportunity he was looking for. He denounced Hitler and the Nazis in the plainest language and told Americans they would have to prepare to defend themselves. More subtly, even deceptively, he arranged the transfer of fifty old destroyers from the American navy to the British fleet, in order that the British keep their sea-lanes open. After his election to a precedent-shattering third term in 1940—an election made possible only by the war—Roosevelt ramped up the aid to Britain, and to other countries fighting Germany and its allies. The Lend-Lease program, approved by Congress in April 1941, supplied weapons, vehicles and other essentials to the defenders of democracy—or the opponents of fascism, whichever description fit best.

Lend-Lease proved the power of the American economy, which eventually provisioned the armies of the United States, Britain, the Soviet Union and China, in addition to several lesser Allied belligerents. It also revealed what Roosevelt had learned about American finance and politics during the 1920s and 1930s. American aid to allies in World War I had taken the form of loans, which had become a source of the financial and political disputes of the interwar decades. Roosevelt deliberately blurred the issue of whether the aid in World War II was a gift or a loan. The crucial thing, he said, was to get the guns, tanks, trucks and planes to whoever happened to be fighting the fascists. Repayment and kindred issues, including the role of the dollar in the postwar settlement, could be considered later.

THE VIEW FROM
MOUNT WASHINGTON

1944–1963

T he consideration began in earnest in the summer of
1944. Seven hundred delegates from the forty-five
nations composing the antifascist alliance gathered at
the Mount Washington Hotel in Bretton Woods, New Hamp-
shire. For decades the hotel had offered a respite from the
sweltering summers of eastern cities, but like many American resorts it had lapsed into premature senility during the
depression of the 1930s. The war compounded the problem by
restricting gasoline supplies and otherwise curtailing travel.
The proprietors looked forward to the end of the war and the
resumption, they hoped, of previous holiday habits. Already
business was picking up; the summer of 1944 had brought
numerous new bookings. But then the world's public financiers
commandeered the place for three weeks starting in early July.
The American delegation, predictably, was the largest, total-
ing nearly two hundred. The Chinese delegation, curiously,
came second, with forty. The press corps comprised seventy
writers and photographers, although these, with some of the
official delegates, had to find lodgings in spillover inns and
cottages down the road. The cleaning and painting crews had
worked frantically to get the old place in shape; they started at
the roofline and worked toward the ground, with the result that

the guests with the highest-numbered rooms slept and dressed in style and comfort, while those of lesser order maneuvered around drop cloths and mop buckets.

Franklin Roosevelt sent greetings from Washington. The subject of the conference, he said, was vital to the well-being of men and women everywhere. "It concerns the basis on which they will be able to exchange with one another the natural riches of the earth and the products of their own industry and ingenuity." He urged the delegates to undo the damage the world depression had done to international trade. "Commerce is the life blood of a free society. We must see to it that the arteries which carry that blood stream are not clogged again, as they have been in the past, by artificial barriers created through senseless economic rivalries." Roosevelt implored the delegates to think beyond the borders of their own countries. Others may have noted the irony of such a plea from the president who in 1933 had scuttled the London economic conference and wrecked hopes for an international approach to the depression, but Roosevelt indicated neither memory nor remorse as he said, "Economic diseases are highly communicable. It follows, therefore, that the economic health of every country is a proper matter of concern to all its neighbors, near and distant. . . . The things that we need to do must be done—can only be done—in concert."

Henry Morgenthau amplified Roosevelt's message. The treasury secretary headed the American delegation and served as Roosevelt's man on the ground. "I hope that this conference will focus its attention upon two elementary economic axioms," he said. "The first of these is this: that prosperity has no fixed limits. It is not a finite substance to be diminished by division. On the contrary, the more of it that other nations enjoy, the more each nation will have for itself." The opposite of this view had prompted the trade wars of the 1930s, whose disastrous outcome was too well known. "The second axiom is a corollary of the first," Morgenthau continued. "Prosperity, like peace, is indivisible. We cannot afford to have it scattered here or there among the fortunate or to enjoy it at the expense of others. Poverty, wherever it exists, is menacing to us all and undermines the well-being of each of us. It can no more be localized than war, but spreads and saps the economic strength of all the most favored areas of the earth." Getting more specific, Morgenthau urged the delegates to devise "a sound currency basis for the balanced growth of international trade . . . a permanent mechanism to promote exchange stability." In addition they should erect a framework for providing the loans that would be required to rebuild the economies blasted by the war. An "international bank for postwar reconstruction" could serve as the foundation.

The delegates took Roosevelt and Morgenthau seriously, less because of the power of their arguments than because of the strength of the dollar. The end of the war wasn't quite in view, but the shape of the postwar world was plain enough. America's principal economic competitors would be bankrupt (Britain), demoralized (France) or destroyed (Germany and Japan). The dollar had reigned as the world's first currency for a generation, but now it would rule. The German mark and the Japanese yen were finished; the British pound and the French franc were on Lend-Lease life support. Lend-Lease might outlast the war but not for long; the survival of the British and French economies would require a new suffusion of dollars.

The strength of the dollar allowed the American government to dictate to the Bretton Woods conference. The delegates gathered early each morning and talked all day, often continuing long past dark. Everyone found the pace of the work demanding. Mabel Newcomer, the head of the economics department at Vassar College, the only woman on the American delegation and a noted mountain climber, was asked by a reporter whether she had found time to test her skills on the upper reaches of Mount Washington. "Last night the American delegation met until midnight," she answered. "I haven't much time for mountaineering." John Maynard Keynes, heading the British delegation, found the pace exhausting. "Keynes thought that the pressure was 'quite unbelievable,' though by our standards it did not seem unusual," the American assistant secretary of state for economic affairs, Dean Acheson, recalled. The regimen almost killed Keynes, who suffered a heart attack near the end of the conference. The Americans and British tried to keep the matter quiet, lest observers and the financial markets take fright. But the papers got the word, prompting close Anglo-American scrutiny of any who might have wanted to sabotage the conference by leaking the news. The explanation was more prosaic. "It appeared that on the evening of his attack an alarmed Lady Keynes, looking for someone to fetch a doctor, found a most helpful young man who, of course, turned out to have been a newspaper correspondent," Acheson explained.

Consensus came hard, despite the American dominance—or perhaps because of it. The conferees didn't want to succumb to the inevitable any sooner than necessary. The conference ran past its stated deadline, compelling the proprietors of the hotel to wire eager guests to stay home a few more days. But on July 22 the conferees unveiled the results of their endeavors. They proclaimed an International Bank for Reconstruction and Development, which would channel postwar aid to the neediest countries. The basic principle of this institution, which quickly came to be called the World Bank, was the internationalization of aid. The bitterness that had surrounded the bilateral lending and repayment schemes of the 1920s would be mitigated by the many fingerprints on the reconstruction and development loans. To be sure, the American fingerprints would be more distinctive and numerous than those from other countries, because the United States would provide the largest contribution to the World Bank's capital. And the loans would typically be in the form of dollars. Moreover, the World Bank would be headquartered in Washington. Still, the international character of the bank diminished the visibility of the United States in the whole undertaking.

The second institution created at Bretton Woods was the International Monetary Fund. The purpose of the fund, in the words of its charter, was "to promote exchange stability, to maintain orderly exchange arrangements among members, and to avoid competitive exchange depreciation." As a first step toward the desired exchange stability, the conference reestablished the international gold standard, with a dollarized twist. "The par value of the currency of each member shall be expressed in terms of gold as a common denominator or in terms of the United States dollar of the weight and fineness in effect on July 1, 1944," the Bretton Woods accord proclaimed. The dollar described was the one established by Congress ten years before, pegging the dollar to gold at $35 per ounce. Members' currencies could rise or fall in value but only within narrow limits. "No member shall buy gold at a price above par value plus the prescribed margin, or sell gold at a price below par value minus the prescribed margin."

Perhaps it wasn't the rigorous schedule that provoked Keynes's heart attack; perhaps it was his knowledge that Bretton Woods marked the definitive eclipse of Britain and the pound sterling by America and the dollar. It remained literally true that the sun never set on Britain's empire, but metaphorically the fiery ball had already splashed into a sea of British red ink. The dollar kept the empire afloat and would continue to do so as long as American leaders, the new masters of the world order, permitted. Keynes had been born in 1882, in the salad days of British economic and imperial power; he would die in 1946, just before the tempest of decolonization stripped Britain of most of its far-flung territories. But the pound had already become a secondary currency, linked like all the rest to the dominant dollar.

The dollar's dominion expanded and ramified after the war. Casual observers thought American hegemony rested on American military might, stunningly exemplified by the atomic blasts that brought Japan to its knees three months after the German surrender. But American military power was a declining asset; no sooner had the war ended than American

GIs and their families began clamoring for the government to demobilize the troops. Harry Truman, unexpectedly president after Franklin Roosevelt's sudden death, resisted the clamor for a time, but by 1946 American military power was fading fast. The atomic bomb lent an appearance of continuing military might, but there were fewer bombs in the arsenal than anyone on the outside—as well as most on the inside—knew, and in any case American strategists had difficulty identifying circumstances under which American leaders might actually use the horrible weapons.

The dollar, by contrast, was a strengthening asset. The dollar made possible the embrace by the American people of the most radical part of the government's postwar program. Freer trade had been a Democratic cause for decades, but most of those decades had been Republican ones in which the Democrats advocated the removal of barriers to international commerce but accomplished little to knock them down. Roosevelt and the New Deal Democrats had chipped at the frowning edifice of the Smoot-Hawley tariff but were constrained from doing more by the inward-looking politics of the era—to which Roosevelt, of course, had contributed significantly. The war, however, compelled an outward American look, and the war's end enabled Roosevelt and his Democratic successors to indulge their open-door propensities.

Even so, free trade wouldn't have caught on without an assurance that it would work to America's advantage. Early proponents of protective American tariffs had asserted the need to coddle infant firms, but by 1945 American firms were industrial giants. In that year American factories churned out more steel, railroad equipment, machine tools and other industrial products than the rest of the world combined. The only industries that required coddling were those in other countries. Yet the dollar's power was such that Washington, with the shoe now firmly on the other foot, could insist on market-opening measures.

The delegates at Bretton Woods had informally discussed

an international organization to undo the damage of the trade wars of the 1930s and prevent their repetition, but the concept took institutional hold only with the 1947 inauguration of the General Agreements on Tariffs and Trade. The GATT provided the framework for a series of negotiations—called "rounds" and named for the cities where they occurred—with the purpose of reducing tariffs and other barriers to trade. The work proceeded slowly at times but always in the direction of freer trade.

The result was a closer knitting of international markets and a consequent diminution of the trade-triggered hostilities that had plagued the 1930s. In this respect the new economic order confirmed Roosevelt's prediction that peace would follow commerce. Countries and peoples that had just finished fighting each other to the bloody death became one another's best customers. The same border crossings through which convoys of tanks had recently rolled now saw convoys of trucks carrying consumer goods.

A second result was the cementing of the dollar's hegemony. The United States was the only major country whose economy exited the war in better shape than it entered; the goods that flowed across the newly opening borders carried the label "Made in USA" more often than the label of any other country. American economists and elected officials had worried that the end of the war might trigger a return to high domestic unemployment as government spending on war materiel ceased and twelve million soldiers reentered the civilian workforce. Dean Acheson, testifying before Congress, identified converting the economy from war to peace as the most important problem facing the country. "If we do not do that," Acheson said, "it seems clear that we are in for a very bad time, so far as the economic and social position of the country is concerned." Crucial to the conversion was the opening of foreign markets. "No group which has ever studied this problem, and there have been many . . . ," Acheson told Congress, "has ever believed that our domestic markets could absorb our entire production under our present system. You must look to foreign markets."

The dollar-centric regime of Bretton Woods and the GATT ensured American producers access to foreign markets, and the feared recurrence of the depression didn't materialize. The American economy hiccupped during the transition from war to peace, but soon it surged ahead at a rate not seen in peacetime since the 1920s. Consumers spent the savings they had accumulated during the war, when patriotism and rationing curtailed consumption, and American exporters captured markets the trade wars of the 1930s and the real war of the 1940s had prevented them from reaching.

And when some of those markets developed more slowly than American manufacturers, workers and shippers thought proper, the American government gave them a boost. The European Recovery Program originated in a 1947 commencement speech by Secretary of State George Marshall at Harvard University. The war had ravaged the continent, which still bore the scars of the conflict, Marshall said. "Machinery has fallen into disrepair or is entirely obsolete. Long-standing commercial ties, private institutions, banks, insurance companies, and shipping companies disappeared through loss of capital, absorption through nationalization, or by simple destruction. In many countries confidence in the local currency has been severely shaken." Food and fuel were in short supply; the winter just ending had been the harshest in memory. Millions wondered whether, having survived the war, they would survive the peace. Marshall told his audience, on that happy June day in Cambridge, that conditions across the Atlantic could hardly be more perilous. "The truth of the matter is that Europe's requirements for the next three or four years of foreign food and other essential products—principally from America—are so much greater than her present ability to pay that she must have substantial additional help or face economic, social, and political deterioration of a very grave character."

The necessary response, Marshall said, was a major program of American aid. "The United States should do whatever it is able to do to assist in the return of normal economic health in the world. . . . Such assistance, I am convinced, must not be on a piecemeal basis as various crises develop. Any assistance that this government may render in the future should provide a cure rather than a mere palliative." Marshall added, "Our policy is directed not against any country or doctrine but against hunger, poverty, desperation, and chaos."

Marshall felt obliged to utter this last line because it was so patently untrue. By 1947 the awkward comity of the war years between the United States and the Soviet Union had dissolved into the armed hostility of the Cold War. American leaders worried that Europeans might conclude that democratic capitalism could not furnish the necessities of a decent existence and turn in anger or despair to communism. Marshall's plan was directed toward the people of Europe, but it was also directed against the Soviet Union and the doctrine of communism.

Marshall's brief persuaded Congress, which provided more than $12 billion over the next several years for the recovery the secretary described. The aid came with strings. The Europeans had to coordinate their economic policies to ensure that the money not be wasted in needless competition. And most of the money had to be spent in the United States. The money wasn't a loan—it didn't have to be repaid—but neither was it a gift. It was rather a massive system of credits applicable to American products, which would then be transported to Europe in American ships.

The plan was a brilliant trifecta. The billions of dollars underwrote the continued expansion of the American economy; the materials the dollars purchased facilitated the recovery of Europe; the recovery instilled hope that held communism at bay.

Yet the dollar's very success in promoting economic revival planted the seeds of challenge to the dollar's hegemony. In Germany the revival took the form of the *Wirtschaftswunder*, or economic miracle, by which the Germans regained the dynamism and productivity that for decades had made them such a force in Europe. The new West German currency, the deutschemark, gained respectability under the watchful eye and rigid discipline of the Bonn government. A comparable revival, funded not by Marshall Plan money but by spillover spending from the Korean War, put Japan back in business. The Japanese, building on a smaller prewar base than Germany, trailed the Germans in most measures of economic strength, but they, like the Germans, served notice on the world that the dollar wouldn't have its way forever.

Another development suggested the same thing. The coordination George Marshall had demanded as a condition of American aid to Europe gave rise to the European Coal and Steel Community, a pooling of the heavy industries of Germany, France, Italy, Belgium, the Netherlands and Luxembourg. The coal and steel community ramified into the larger European Economic Community, often called the Common Market, which mimicked the secret of the American dollar's early success: the existence of a large internal market for American products. The Common Market encouraged trade among members, allowing firms in each country to expand to optimal economic size, unconstrained by the political borders that heretofore had held them in. Politics didn't disappear; France kept Britain out of the Common Market until the 1970s. But politics no longer played the central role it once had, and the European economies flourished.

Meanwhile American self-confidence and ambitions continued to grow. The emergence of a Europe worth defending caused a critical mass of Americans, including two-thirds of the Senate, to put aside their country's long-standing aversion to peacetime alliances and endorse the North Atlantic Treaty of 1949. The North Atlantic Treaty begot the North Atlantic Treaty Organization, which featured an integrated military command. The United States naturally took the lead in NATO, paying most of its expenses and providing most of its troops. American forces took up permanent residence in Germany,

France and other NATO countries, the better to deter a Soviet attack. Washington provided security guarantees to countries beyond Europe as well, including Japan, Taiwan, South Korea and Pakistan. The American commitment to Vietnam occurred more gradually but no less portentously, with the United States taking the place of France as the guarantor of South Vietnam against communist North Vietnam.

In ancient and early modern times empires were expected to pay for themselves. Persia and Rome exacted tribute from their vassal states; Britain extracted profits, initially via the East India Company, from its domain in South Asia. Whether the realm of influence America created in the 1940s and 1950s constituted an empire evoked debate, but even if it did, it differed from those previous empires in that it cost Americans much more than it returned. Yet Americans paid the bill, believing that the future of democracy depended on battling communism wherever that noxious ideology reared its head. The more zealous likened the struggle to a crusade; others considered the containment of communism akin to the purchase of an insurance policy. It is the rich who purchase insurance, since they can afford the premiums and have the most to lose. Americans in the 1950s felt rich enough to buy plenty of insurance.

The dollar built America's allies up, but it could also knock them to their knees. As the Cold War rivalry between the United States and the Soviet Union split Europe and parts of Asia into two camps, a third camp—a "third world"—self-consciously carved a zone for itself apart from both. India's Jawaharlal Nehru and Yugoslavia's Josip Broz Tito were founding fathers of the neutralist movement; Egypt's Gamal Abdel Nasser joined as quickly as he could. Nasser angled for maximum influence for himself and Egypt by playing the United States against the Soviet Union in the matter of economic aid. The American administration of Dwight Eisenhower abruptly pulled back, leaving Nasser short of funding for a new Nile dam at Aswan; Nasser responded by nationalizing the Suez Canal Company and earmarking the tolls for the dam.

The seizure irked Eisenhower but sent Anthony Eden, the British prime minister, over the edge. The canal had long been Britain's lifeline to India, and though India was no longer part of Britain's formal empire, British trade with India and the oil states of the Persian Gulf passed through the canal. The British government, moreover, as a major shareholder in the canal company, counted on the tolls to help balance its budget. Eden quietly vowed that Nasser would be made to disgorge his theft, and the prime minister concocted a scheme for toppling the Egyptian leader. Britain combined with France and Israel, which had their own reasons for distrusting Nasser, to land an expeditionary force in Egypt near the canal.

Eden thought Eisenhower would welcome the operation or at least tacitly accept it. Consequently he was shocked when Eisenhower stood stoutly against it. The president didn't want the United States associated with what seemed to most of the world a throwback to the evil days of overt imperialism. He realized, moreover, that the Soviet Union would move quickly to exploit NATO embarrassment in the Middle East.

Eisenhower registered his disapproval diplomatically at the United Nations but with greater force economically. The Suez invasion prompted a run on the British pound as investors sought stronger currencies, starting with the dollar. Since Bretton Woods the United States, as the linchpin of the world system, had intervened directly or through the International Monetary Fund to defend endangered currencies. Eden and the British, enamored of their "special relationship" with the Americans, not unreasonably expected Eisenhower to come to the aid of the pound.

Eisenhower refused. He thought Eden was being stupid, and he resented the prime minister's attempt to foist a fait accompli on him. "Nothing justifies double-crossing us," Eisenhower angrily told an assistant. He made clear that Britain could expect no help from the United States until the invasion force was withdrawn. "We meet a brick wall at every turn with the administration," a British diplomat in Washington wrote home. "The attitude of the administration can best be summed up by 'you have got yourselves into this mess, now get yourselves out of it.'"

Eisenhower's opposition brought the Suez invasion to a shuddering halt. The president complemented his financial strong-arm with a stern rejection of British pleas to send emergency oil to Britain to make up for shortfalls in shipments from the Middle East. The double blow stunned Eden and shortly drove him from office.

The whole affair deeply scarred the British psyche. During the decade since the war most Britons had accepted intellectually that the empire and the pound were no longer what they had been. But not till the wrenching week of Suez did the emotional meaning of Britain's decline sink in. The country's once-proud currency had fallen hostage to the upstart dollar; from such financial weakness the humiliation of the empire ineluctably ensued.

John Kennedy inherited the dollar's dominion from Eisenhower, along with the costs of maintaining that dominion. "For the past decade our international transactions have resulted in a deficit—payments that were in excess of receipts— in every year except that of the Suez crisis," Kennedy informed the American people in 1961. More dollars were going out than were coming in, and while the imbalance could persist for a while, it couldn't go on forever. Sooner or later the country would run out of dollars. The United States still ran a trade surplus, exporting more than it imported, but the trade surplus didn't equal the sum of American military expenditures abroad, American overseas investment and American foreign aid. These outlays were necessary, Kennedy said. Defense spending protected the country; capital investment preserved trade and employment; foreign aid supported America's friends in the struggle against communism. Even so, they added up.

And they were taking a toll on the dollar. Of late, foreign dollar-holders had been redeeming their notes for gold, with the result being a large drain of the yellow metal from American reserves. There was no cause for alarm—yet. "Our gold reserve now stands at $17.5 billion," Kennedy said. "This is more than one-and-a-half times foreign official dollar holdings and more than 90 percent of all foreign dollar holdings. It is some two-fifths of the gold stock of the entire free world." The dollar remained as firmly attached to gold as ever. "The United States official dollar price of gold can and will be maintained at $35 an ounce." The government would defend this price. "Those who fear weakness in the dollar will find their fears unfounded. Those who hope for speculative reasons for an increase in the price of gold will find their hopes in vain."

But Kennedy wouldn't have raised the issue if it weren't cause for concern, and he declared that Americans needed to put their financial house in order. He directed the Pentagon to jawbone America's allies into contributing to the upkeep of American forces abroad. He advocated a variety of steps by various agencies of the government to boost exports. "These measures," he said, "combined with increasing confidence in the dollar abroad and steady economic growth at home, can cure the basic long-term deficit in our balance of payments and check the outflow of gold."

Yet Kennedy's efforts proved insufficient, and the balance of payments tipped further against the United States. The shortfall became his chronic headache. "The problems posed by our balance of payments deficits over the last several years are neither easily understood nor quickly solved," he wrote David Rockefeller, the president of Chase Manhattan Bank, in 1962. Rockefeller was his generation's closest approximation to J. P. Morgan; Kennedy wrote to him as to the representative of the financial community at large, which was getting nervous about the dollar's future. Kennedy sought to soothe the nerves. He promised that the government would bring the payments deficit under control and maintain the dollar's strength and credibility. "This country will not—I repeat not—increase the price of gold, thereby devaluating the dollar," he told Rockefeller. The administration would twist foreign arms even harder to get support for the dollar. "We know we cannot solve this problem alone—and other free nations know that they, too, cannot afford any weakness in the dollar, which is the very foundation of the international monetary system." Rockefeller and the financial community should keep faith in the dollar. "I assure you that this Administration intends to do whatever must be done to make certain that the dollar remains as 'sound as a dollar.'"

≡ FLOATING, FLOATING . . . ≡

1963–1973

K ennedy bequeathed the payments deficit and the dollar-doubting it evoked to Lyndon Johnson, who tried to make it better but merely made it worse. Johnson stretched the federal budget to cover both the domestic programs that constituted his Great Society and the foreign war—in Vietnam—that constituted his great mistake. Federal spending grew by half from 1964 to 1968, federal revenues by substantially less. The resulting budget deficit, of $25 billion by 1968, combined with continuing balance-of-payments troubles to produce inflationary pressure that caused investors and foreign governments to gravely doubt the dollar's ability to carry the weight of the world on its shoulders, as the Bretton Woods system required.

Charles de Gaulle didn't doubt the dollar so much as resent it. The French president had long bridled under the dollar's hegemony, which he considered insulting to French *grandeur*. "American imperialism, no domain escapes it," he told an associate. "It takes all shapes, but the most insidious is that of the dollar." What made the dollar's hold the more infuriating was America's fiscal ineptitude. "The United States is not capable of balancing its budget," de Gaulle said. "It allows itself to have enormous debts. Since the dollar is the reference currency everywhere, it can use others to suffer the effects of its poor management. It exports its inflation all over the world. This is not acceptable. This cannot last."

De Gaulle challenged the dollar's primacy. In February 1965 he held an elaborate press conference at the Elysée Palace, where he called for an end to the Bretton Woods system and a return to the traditional gold standard. "We consider it necessary to put international exchange on a monetary base that is indisputable and which carries the stamp of no country in particular, as was the case before the world's great upheavals," he said. De Gaulle knew the United States would oppose his effort, but he thought the Americans should taste their own medicine. "Many global companies are expropriated for the benefit of Americans, with capital they get from their inflation," he asserted privately. He predicted of American officials: "They will react, but that doesn't matter very much."

De Gaulle's rhetorical attack delighted his French supporters. "Journalists are split between the dazzle of this brilliant lecture, the stupor of seeing this military man leap into a technical subject he should not know anything about, and the irony of seeing him go merrily against the dollar fortress, unassailable by definition," de Gaulle's information minister observed.

The French president put teeth into his words by demanding gold in exchange for France's dollars. The redemption strained the American treasury, as de Gaulle intended it to do; it also compelled Johnson to consider modifications to the Bretton Woods system, as de Gaulle similarly intended. In public Johnson still defended Bretton Woods, and he denounced the traditional gold standard. "To go back to a system based on gold alone—to a system which brought us all to disaster in the early 1930s—is not an answer the world would, or should, accept," he said. And he promised he would not retreat from America's commitments. "The United States will continue to meet its international monetary responsibilities. I reaffirm unequivocally the commitment of the United States to buy and sell gold at the existing price of $35 an ounce."

Yet Johnson simultaneously took a first step toward undermining that commitment. By 1968 the scores of billions of dollars held by foreigners seriously threatened the ability of the American government to convert them to gold on demand. The problem was America's, but it was also the world's, in that doubts about America's ability to convert crimped the international financial system. The Johnson administration worked out an arrangement with America's partners in the International Monetary Fund to create a kind of paper gold, called special drawing rights. "They will perform the same basic function in the international monetary system as gold, dollars, or other reserve currencies," Johnson explained in a message to Congress. The new assets would be distributed according to each country's quota with the IMF; the United States, as the largest funder, would receive the largest share of the new assets. Johnson hastened to assert—less than believably—that the special drawing rights represented not a retreat from Bretton Woods but a completion of the Bretton Woods system. "The very success of the system in stimulating trade has put new pressures on the Bretton Woods machinery and shows us how that machinery must now be changed." The special drawing rights would extend the life of the machinery. And they would extend the healthy life of the dollar. "A strong dollar is essential to the stability of the international financial structure," Johnson concluded.

But the paper gold merely papered over the problem, which Richard Nixon in turn inherited from Johnson. Nixon benefited from a briefly balanced budget—the result of a tax surcharge from Johnson's final year in office—but Americans imported increasingly more than they exported, magnifying the balance-of-payments deficit. Foreigners redeemed more and more dollars for gold, depleting the American treasury. Nixon's treasury secretary, John Connally, took the matter personally. "Foreigners are out to screw us," he said. "Our job is to screw them first." Connally informed America's trading partners how this philosophy applied to the dollar: "The dollar may be our currency, but it's your problem."

Connally's confrontational posture lasted until the middle of 1971. That August the president summoned his economic team to Camp David for a confidential meeting. Speechwriter William Safire caught a helicopter ride from Washington with Herbert Stein, the chairman of the Council of Economic Advisers. Safire asked Stein what the meeting was about. Stein couldn't say for certain, but he knew it was significant. "This could be the most important weekend in the history of economics since March 4, 1933," he said. Safire racked his brain, finally summoning Franklin Roosevelt's bank holiday. "We're closing the banks?" he asked Stein. "Hardly," Stein replied. "But I would not be surprised if the president were to close the gold window." Safire was no economist, and he didn't know what the gold window was or what closing it meant. But neither did he want to confess his ignorance. En route to Camp David he sat beside a midlevel treasury official who asked if Safire had been told the purpose of the meeting. Safire nonchalantly replied that the president might close the gold window. "My God!" the treasury man said, cradling his head in his hands. Safire guessed he ought to find out what closing the window meant. He asked Stein. "It's the suspension of the convertibility of the dollar," Stein shouted over the noise of the helicopter. Safire continued his bluff. "Anybody knows *that*, but how would you put it in one-syllable words?" he shouted back. Stein looked at Safire as if to gauge the depth of his economic ignorance. "*I* wouldn't," he said.

Nixon swore the group to secrecy as soon as they arrived at the presidential retreat. "There are to be absolutely no calls made out of here," he said. "Between now and Monday night, everyone here is to button his lip." Nixon proceeded to explain why he had gathered them all. "We are here to find solutions. We have to test ideas as to whether they will work. We have to test the cosmetic effect—to limit the consequences. It is easy to take spectacular action—and this will be the most significant economic action since World War II. The question is, how do you get out from under it if it doesn't work?"

John Connally soon made clear that cosmetics were the issue to be discussed. The treasury secretary presented the substance of the meeting as a fait accompli. "We have to close the gold window," he said. This first step would halt the drain on gold at once. "We should seriously consider an import tax, in the range of 10 to 15 percent," Connally continued. This second step would help correct the trade imbalance. "The final step should be imposition of a wage and price freeze until January 1, 1972." He turned from the broader group to speak to the president. "If you do this, the international financial people will realize you moved across the board strongly. This would be acting in consonance with the way people view you—great statesmanship and great courage."

Arthur Burns, the Federal Reserve director, agreed. Burns was far closer to Nixon than most Fed chiefs have been to the presidents they worked alongside; Burns's critics claimed he sold out the Fed to the White House. On this day he congratulated the president on his projected boldness. "These actions will electrify the world," Burns said. But he warned that the president's many critics would find fault. "Never mind if it's right or wrong—consider how it will be exploited by the politicians," he said. The communists would certainly pile on. "I could write the editorial in *Pravda*: 'The Disintegration of Capitalism.'" America's allies would be little happier. "Once the dollar floats, the basis for trade changes," Burns said. "I would fear retaliation by other countries."

Nixon agreed that he would face criticism. "The media will be vicious," he said. But that was how the politics of international finance was played. "If I were on the other side I would do the same thing. I would kick our balls off."

Paul Volcker, the treasury undersecretary for international monetary affairs, urged circumspection upon the group.

"Everybody who speculates in gold will seize on this to make a mint," he said. Perhaps the administration should deliberately fool the gold speculators. "Maybe we should sell some."

Nixon took Volcker's point in a slightly different direction. "I want this kept secret," he reiterated. "The one thing that is sure to come on this is, why didn't we tell the press beforehand?" Nixon imagined how he might reply to such a question: "Why you dumb bastards, if we told you, you would have told the world, and we would have lost all our gold."

Volcker nodded. "Fortunes could be made with this information," he said.

H. R. Haldeman, Nixon's chief of staff, demanded, "How? Exactly?"

Volcker turned to George Shultz, the director of the Office of Management and Budget. "How much is your deficit?" Volcker asked.

"Twenty-three billion dollars," Shultz said.

"Give me a billion dollars and a free hand on Monday," Volcker said, "and I'll make it for you on the money market."

Nixon set William Safire to work on a speech but then wrote a partial rough draft himself. "Let me lay to rest the bugaboo of devaluation," he said. "Will this action reduce the value of the dollar? The long-term purpose and effect of this action will be to strengthen the dollar, not weaken it. Short term, the dollar will buy less. But you overwhelming majority who buy American products in America, your dollar will be worth the same tomorrow as it is today."

Nixon had intended to spring his surprise on the world on Monday, August 16, but decided that the markets would wonder what was going on at Camp David and probably react poorly. So he took to the air on Sunday night, the 15th. "The time has come for a new economic policy for the United States," Nixon said. "Its targets are unemployment, inflation, and international speculation." The policy would tackle unemployment by means of a tax cut and an investment tax credit. It would target inflation by cuts in federal spending and by a wage and price freeze.

And it would deal with speculation by a dramatic restructuring of American and world finance. "In the past seven years, there has been an average of one international monetary crisis every year," Nixon said. "Now, who gains from these crises? Not the workingman; not the investor; not the real producers of wealth. The gainers are the international money speculators. Because they thrive on crises, they help to create them. In recent weeks, the speculators have been waging an all-out war on the American dollar." The U.S. government had no choice but to safeguard the dollar, the president said. "I have directed Secretary Connally to suspend temporarily the convertibility of the dollar into gold or other reserve assets."

Nixon said he expected criticism. "This action will not win us any friends among the international money traders," he said. But his care lay elsewhere. "Our primary concern is with the American workers, and with fair competition around the world. . . . I am determined that the American dollar must never again be a hostage in the hands of international speculators." Nixon avoided mention of Bretton Woods by name, but he praised the historic accomplishments of the postwar system of finance. "At the end of World War II the economies of the major industrial nations of Europe and Asia were shattered. To help them get on their feet and to protect their freedom, the United States has provided over the past twenty-five years $143 billion in foreign aid. . . . Today, largely with our help, they have regained their vitality. They have become our strong competitors, and we welcome their success." But success brought responsibility. "Now that other nations are economically strong, the time has come for them to bear their fair share of the burden of defending freedom around the world. The time has come for exchange rates to be set straight and for the major nations to compete as equals. There is no longer any need for the United States to compete with one hand tied behind her back."

Nixon dismantled Bretton Woods in a weekend; building a replacement took decades. The work began in the months after Nixon's August surprise. By closing the gold window the president broke one of the two chains of the Bretton Woods monetary system, the one linking the dollar to gold. America's partners in the system subsequently saw little reason to maintain the other chain, the one connecting their currencies to the dollar. Neither did Nixon: the point of detaching from gold was to devalue the dollar against the currencies of America's trade partners.

But enough of the Bretton Woods spirit remained that the big financial powers desired an orderly transition from the old order to the new. Nixon brought their finance ministers to Washington in December 1971. The Group of Ten huddled at the Smithsonian Institution and ratified the revaluations the international money markets had already imposed on the major currencies. The dollar was devalued some 15 percent against the German mark and the Japanese yen, and a wider slippage band was allowed. The dollar was reattached to gold, but at $38 per ounce rather than $35.

Nixon put the best face on his financial revolution. "Bretton Woods came at a time when the United States, immediately after World War II, was predominant in economic affairs in the world and the decision of the United States was, perhaps, the most important one to be made at that time," the president extemporized to a television audience. "Now we have a new world, fortunately a much better world economically, where instead of just one strong economic nation, the nations of Europe, Japan and Asia, Canada and North America, all of these nations are strong economically, strong competitors." Nixon didn't call them America's equals; they hadn't achieved that exalted status. But he acknowledged their partnership and the influence they brought to the negotiating table. "The fact that these gentlemen, over a period of weeks, finally culminating in the last two days, have reached agreement on the realignment of exchange rates, is, indeed, the most significant event that has occurred in world financial history." Nixon acknowledged that international finance was a competitive arena;

people would want to know who had won and who lost in the dramatic reordering of affairs. The answer was: "The whole free world has won."

Perhaps the free world agreed, but the free market didn't. The dollar's devaluation under the Smithsonian agreement bought time but not satisfaction; the pressures that had driven Nixon to close the gold window mounted again. The accord Nixon hailed as the most significant in history lasted mere months. Britain detached the pound from the dollar; Germany loosed the mark. Nixon agreed to another devaluation, repricing the dollar at $42 per ounce of gold. Yet even this line couldn't be held, and in March 1973 he and the leaders of the other financial powers agreed to let their currencies float against one another. Henceforth markets, not governments, would determine the value of currencies. The dollar became but one of several competitors for the favor of traders.

PETRODOLLARS,
EURODOLLARS AND
THE INVINCIBLE YEN

1973–1989

The dust from the rubble of Bretton Woods had scarcely settled when Nixon discovered, and the world with him, that another mineral resource had an even greater impact than gold on the value of the dollar. Ever since oil had first been produced commercially in the nineteenth century, supply had generally outstripped demand. Fresh discoveries chronically caused the price to collapse; during the 1930s in the big new field of East Texas, oil for a time was literally cheaper than water. Various methods were employed to boost the price of oil. The Texas Railroad Commission, which for historic reasons regulated oil in the Lone Star State, set production quotas that curtailed supply and lifted prices—not simply in Texas but, because Texas was such a dominant producer, in the world, giving the three-person Texas panel inordinate and often unappreciated power over the global economy. In 1960 several major oil-producing nations banded together in the Organization of the Petroleum Exporting Countries, which soon attracted other members. For the first decade of its existence OPEC operated primarily as a trade association, sparring with the big multinational oil companies over concessions and royalties, but in the early 1970s its influence increased dramatically. Growth in consumption had narrowed the gap between supply and demand. The United States, for decades the swing producer in world supplies, no longer had the spare capacity to cover surges in demand. "We feel this to be a historic occasion," the chairman of the Texas Railroad Commission declared in March 1971, when the commission authorized production at full capacity for the first time since World War II. "Damned historic, and a sad one. Texas oil fields have been like a reliable old warrior that could rise to the task when needed. That old warrior can't rise anymore."

What rose in the warrior's place was OPEC. The balance of oil power shifted to the Persian Gulf, where OPEC members Saudi Arabia, Iraq, Kuwait and Iran sat on a subterranean sea of petroleum, which suddenly afforded them enormous leverage over the world economy. The United States, historically an oil exporter, became vulnerable to OPEC's manipulations as Americans began consuming more oil than they produced. Nonproducing Europe and Japan were even more vulnerable.

The OPEC countries didn't take long to flex their new muscle. Nixon's devaluation of the dollar had hit the oil producers hard, as world oil was priced in dollars. "What is the point of producing more oil and selling it for an unguaranteed paper currency?" the oil minister of Kuwait asked. "Why produce the oil which is my bread and butter and strength and exchange it for a sum of money whose value will fall next year?" His answer, and that of his fellow OPEC ministers, was to produce less oil and sell it for more money. In October 1973 Israel and neighboring Arabs went to war for the fourth time in a quarter-century; the United States, having identified ever more closely with Israel during that quarter-century, backstopped Israel with weapons when the Israelis floundered during the first days of the war. The Arab members of OPEC, from a mix of political solidarity with their frontline cousins and economic opportunism arising from the production-consumption pinch, announced an embargo of oil to the United States.

The embargo evoked panic in world markets. "We weren't bidding just for oil," one refiner explained. "We were bidding for our life." Oil prices spiked upward, quadrupling within weeks. In some places oil and its derivatives couldn't be had for any price. Refiners rationed gasoline to retailers in America; drivers lined up for blocks awaiting their turn at the pump, often to discover that the gas had run out before they got there. Nixon warned the American people to brace for a cold winter. "We are heading toward the most acute shortages of energy since World War II," the president said. "Our supply of petroleum this winter will be at least 10 percent short of our anticipated demands, and it could fall short by as much as 17 percent." Americans would have to adjust their lifestyle to the new reality. "To be sure that there is enough oil to go around for the entire winter, all over the country, it will be essential for all of us to live and work in lower temperatures. We must ask everyone to lower the thermostat in your home by at least 6 degrees so that we can achieve a national daytime average of 68 degrees." With an expression between a smile and a grimace, Nixon added: "Incidentally, my doctor tells me that in a temperature of 66 to 68 degrees, you are really more healthy than when it is 75 to 78, if that is any comfort."

The Arab-Israeli war ended within weeks and the embargo within months, but the higher oil prices persisted. And they inaugurated the worst stretch for the dollar since the Great Depression. Because oil was a feed stock for everything from plastic to perfume to fertilizer, and because everything had to be transported from producers to consumers in oil-burning ships, trains or trucks, the high oil prices magnified the existing inflationary pressure. Prices in the United States leaped 11 percent in 1974 and almost as much in 1975. The inflation rate retreated slightly until 1979, when a second oil shock, triggered by the Iranian revolution, jolted prices upward another 11 percent, and nearly 14 percent the following year.

The inflation of the 1970s sifted debtors and creditors in a manner just the opposite of that of the deflations of the 1890s and 1930s. Debtors delighted to realize that the dollars they had borrowed dearly would be repaid cheaply; with each month that incomes rose, the burden of debt grew lighter. Creditors suffered correspondingly; by the time they got their money back, it couldn't buy nearly what it bought when they loaned it. The creditors' pain might have outweighed the debtors' delight and prompted a change in government policy, given that creditors typically have closer ties to the political system than debtors. But the psychology of inflation was seductive, within limits. Workers received fatter paychecks; merchants got more for their wares; homeowners saw their equity grow. In real terms, adjusted for the dollar's decline in purchasing power, most of them weren't any better off. But in nominal terms, in the numbers they saw and read about, they felt richer.

The ones who felt the inflation most acutely were those on fixed incomes. The elderly were the largest of this group, and though Social Security pensions were adjusted for inflation, private pensions often weren't, and nest eggs gathered over decades of working almost never were. With little opportunity to elevate their incomes, pensioners experienced the declining dollar as a decline in their standard of living. They had lived through the Great Depression and World War II, and they understood what sacrifice entailed. But this was a sacrifice they hadn't expected, and its insidious operation—its stealthy tarnishing of their golden years—was a blow to their spirit.

Most observers saw the inflation of the 1970s as reason for concern; Jimmy Carter judged it cause for alarm. Carter read polls indicating that Americans had lost their natural optimism, and he decided the nation needed a lecture. "I want to talk to you right now about a fundamental threat to American democracy," he said in July 1979. The threat came not from a foreign foe but from within the American people. "It is a crisis of confidence. It is a crisis that strikes at the very heart and soul and spirit of our national will." The previous two decades had been hard on America's sense of self. "We were sure that ours was a nation of the ballot, not the bullet, until the murders of John Kennedy and Robert Kennedy and Martin Luther King,

Jr. We were taught that our armies were always invincible and our causes were always just, only to suffer the agony of Vietnam. We respected the presidency as a place of honor until the shock of Watergate." The inflation of the last several years had compounded the discouragement. "We remember when the phrase 'sound as a dollar' was an expression of absolute dependability, until ten years of inflation began to shrink our dollar and our savings."

The odd thing about what came to be called the "malaise" speech—aside from the fact that Carter didn't utter that word—was that his searching of the American soul was a preface to an essentially prosaic policy of energy conservation. Yet those attuned to financial affairs noticed something else. Carter took two steps that betrayed his own failing confidence in America's future. He usurped the authority, or at least a fundamental prerogative, of the Fed by having his administration, rather than the bank board, announce a rise in the discount rate, to a level unthinkable only a few years before: 9.5 percent. Inflation was out of control and must be halted at any cost, the president seemed to be saying.

His second step was even more fraught. He ordered the treasury to sell bonds denominated not in dollars but in German deutschemarks and Swiss francs. These "Carter bonds" answered the complaints of foreign investors who wondered why they should purchase dollar-denominated federal debt when the dollar's value was eroding so fast. The treasury presented the move as a simple exercise in pragmatism, but the fact that the United States government could no longer count on the world to hold dollars portended evil days for the greenback.

Yet at the same time that Carter was acknowledging the dollar's weakness, he made a decision that did more than anything else that decade to give the currency new strength. Ten days after his malaise speech he announced the nomination of Paul Volcker to chair the Fed. Volcker had gone from Nixon's treasury to the New York Federal Reserve Bank, where he took Benjamin Strong's old job. His steady nerve and firm hand inspired Carter to promote him to the apex of the Fed. "Mr. Volcker has broad economic and financial experience and enjoys an outstanding international reputation," Carter said. "He shares my determination to vigorously pursue the battle against inflation at home and to ensure the strength and stability of the dollar abroad."

Carter got all he asked for in Volcker, who immediately declared war on inflation. He persuaded the Fed board to push up interest rates to shockingly high levels—eventually to more than 20 percent. The shock was no side effect; it was the central point. Volcker observed that businesses, workers and consumers had begun to build inflation into their future plans; he concluded that the only way to change the inflationary mindset was through the equivalent of electroshock therapy. The immediate effect was a derangement of the economy; the "Volcker recession" produced the highest unemployment rates since the 1930s, topping 10 percent in 1981. Volcker himself became extremely unpopular. A columnist for the *Washington Post* reported a hockey game attended by Volcker and several other capital dignitaries. "The evening went well and the hockey fans applauded politely as the celebrities were introduced, except when Volcker's name came up," the columnist wrote. "Then the fans booed." Credit-starved farmers registered their anger against Volcker by driving tractors to Washington and blockading the Fed offices.

Some of Volcker's unpopularity rubbed off on Ronald Reagan, who inherited Volcker from Carter. Americans generally preferred the genial Reagan to the sermonizing Carter, whom they sent back to Georgia in the 1980 election. But as the Volcker anti-inflation medicine took hold, some began having second thoughts. Reagan's Republicans suffered sharp losses in the 1982 congressional races, and Reagan himself grew worried looking forward to the presidential contest in 1984.

But then the inflation fever broke. Volcker's apparent insensitivity to the pain of the recession convinced observers

89

and victims that he would keep interest rates high for as long
as it took to wring the inflation out of the economy; that conviction, once internalized, changed the expectations that fed
the inflation, which then responded to the Volcker treatment.
Inflation tumbled from 13 percent in 1981 to 3 percent in 1983,
allowing Volcker and the Fed to bring interest rates back
down. The economy revived, and relieved voters returned
Reagan to office.

Yet the dollar had problems even Volcker couldn't remedy.
During the Reagan years the nation ran twin deficits that
boded ill for the currency's long-term health. The trade deficit
and the federal budget deficit were indeed twins, in that the
excess dollars Americans sent abroad in payment for imports
returned as loans to cover the gap between federal revenues
and expenditures. The recycling suited the moment, making
American consumers happy, foreign lenders satisfied and the
federal government solvent. But the long-term implications
were troubling. When the treasury covered the federal deficit
by selling bonds to Americans, the debt was a family affair, so
to speak, raising intergenerational issues, perhaps, but nothing
that involved outsiders or directly threatened the strength of
the dollar. Bonds purchased by foreigners were another matter.
Foreigners' interests might diverge from those of Americans;
Japanese or German holders of American debt might decide
they had enough dollars and seek another source of security.
Whether foreign demand for dollars fell slowly or fast, it would
weaken the dollar.

Alan Greenspan understood the problem when he became
Volcker's successor at the Fed in 1987. Years earlier Ayn Rand
had dubbed Greenspan "the Undertaker" for his dark suits and
grave demeanor at her intellectual soirees; Greenspan was too
smitten by the high priestess of unfettered capitalism to object
that he possessed other clothes and a sense of humor. Shortly
after assuming leadership of the Fed, though, he thought he
might become the American economy's undertaker. The stock

and real estate markets had rebounded from the Volcker recession, and inflation was beginning to creep upward again. At his first session with the Fed board, Greenspan orchestrated a half-point increase in the discount rate to signal to speculators that they might wish to pull back.

They did so, more rapidly than Greenspan expected. The stock market skidded 5 percent, then another 10, during the first two weeks of October 1987. On Friday, October 16, the Dow Jones average plunged 108 points. The brokers caught their breath over the weekend only to resume selling on Monday morning. Greenspan was scheduled to address a bankers' group in Dallas that evening; when he left Washington the Dow was already off 200 points. On arrival in Texas the first question he asked his greeter was how the market had closed. "Down five-oh-eight," he was told. "Great!" he answered, thinking the number was 5.08. The look on the Texan's face told him he was off by two orders of magnitude. The market had lost 508 points, the largest one-day loss in history—worse than any single session in the Great Crash of 1929.

Greenspan headed for his hotel and a telephone. He consulted with Fed staff, with Wall Street bankers, with Chicago commodities traders, with California savings-and-loan executives and with anyone else he could reach who might have insight into the current crisis and influence in alleviating it. He wasn't old enough to remember the 1929 crash, but he knew enough about its ugly evolution to appreciate that swift action was imperative. When one of his interlocutors that night suggested that the Fed wait and see how the situation played out, he barked into the phone: "We don't need to wait to see what happens! We *know* what's going to happen. You know what people say about getting shot? You feel like you've been punched, but the trauma is such that you don't feel the pain right away? In twenty-four or forty-eight hours, we're going to be feeling a lot of pain."

The next morning Greenspan took a military jet, dispatched by the White House, back to Washington. Wall Street was panicking; en route from Andrews Air Force Base to the Fed offices Greenspan received word that the directors of the New York Stock Exchange were considering closing the market early. Greenspan had no authority over the exchange but voiced his vehement disapproval. Closing the market would signal a complete loss of confidence, he said. Far better to ride out the damage. The exchange directors decided to keep the market open.

Greenspan didn't cite Benjamin Strong, either then or later, and not being a student of Fed history he might not have made the connection, but his actions followed the script Strong had specified sixty years earlier in the event of a stock crash. "The Federal Reserve, consistent with its responsibilities as the nation's central bank, affirmed today its readiness to serve as a source of liquidity to support the economic and financial system," Greenspan told the press after speaking to the other members of the board. The Fed Open Market Committee directed its brokers to buy treasury bonds in billion-dollar batches, to flood the system with money, just as Strong had said it should. Meanwhile Greenspan, other Fed officials and members of the Reagan administration lectured the nation's bankers on their obligation to keep credit lines open.

The strategy worked. The panic diminished to fright, then to worry, concern and finally calm. The situation stabilized and stocks turned upward again. Within months the market had recovered all the ground it had lost, and more. And Alan Greenspan had won a reputation for brilliant financial leadership.

Americans expected to need brilliant leadership to fend off the most serious challenge to the dollar's hegemony since World War II. And like the fighting in World War II, the challenge took shape in two theaters. The European theater witnessed the emergence of a kind of fifth-column assault on the greenback, in the form of "Eurodollars." This expatriate currency consisted of dollar deposits in foreign banks. The terminology and practice had roots in the early Cold War, when the Soviet Union and China feared a freezing of their dollar assets by the United States government; to preclude this they deposited the dollars in banks in London and other European financial centers beyond Washington's reach. The American balance-of-payments deficit during the 1960s caused the Eurodollar phenomenon to grow and spread; it ramified further during the 1970s as the OPEC states parked a substantial portion of their petrodollars in European banks. The breaking of Bretton Woods eliminated the threat the Eurodollars posed to America's gold reserve, but because they resided beyond the control of the Federal Reserve, they complicated the Fed's efforts to manage the American money supply. The rising American trade deficit of the 1980s confirmed the Eurodollar market as a significant arena of investment and speculation, a shadow zone where the Eurodollars operated as wild cards in American monetary policy.

The Asian theater of the assault on the dollar featured an increasingly powerful Japanese yen. Of World War II's principal losers, Japan had been slower than Germany to regain its economic stride, which had been less powerful than Germany's to begin with. But by the 1970s Japanese goods, long deemed inferior in American markets, had gained a reputation for consistent quality. The oil shocks of that decade made gas-sipping Toyotas and Hondas an appealing alternative to the guzzlers Ford and General Motors produced, and the development of new technologies in consumer electronics helped Sony and Panasonic become household names across America. At a time of the dollar's distress and America's self-doubt, Japan's large and growing trade surplus with the United States pushed the yen higher against the dollar, then higher still, sequentially fostering beliefs that Japan's triumph in the markets of the world was possible, likely, inevitable. Many American parents insisted that their children learn the Japanese language to compete in the Japanese-dominated future. A whole literature projected Japan's eclipse of the United States; books with minor variations on the title and theme

Japan as Number One became required reading in board-rooms and classrooms across the country.

The Japanese read enough of the literature to believe in their own boundless future. They bid up real estate in Tokyo and other cities to surprising, then astonishing, levels. A square meter in the Ginza district of the capital commanded one hundred million yen, or one million dollars. A plausibly incredible estimate valued the grounds of the Imperial Palace—assuming it could have been sold—at more than the worth of all the real estate in California. The Japanese stock market soared to breathtaking heights. The yen flexed its muscles against other currencies, especially the dollar, doubling in value against the greenback. Japan's sudden wealth and mighty currency caused Japanese investors to look overseas for bargains. They snatched up the Rockefeller Center in New York, the Pebble Beach golf resort in California and numerous other American icons. Late-night comics joked and outraged pundits thundered that the losers of World War II had become the victors of the postwar peace. The dollar, the currency that had rescued democracy from Japanese imperialism, appeared to be falling hostage to the invincible yen.

≡ BUBBLE AND BOIL ≡

1990–2002

A nd then, just as the new decade dawned, the Japanese bubble burst. Property prices that had been climbing straight up plunged vertically down, falling by half almost overnight and by nine-tenths or more in certain districts before long. The Nikkei stock market index dove from 40,000 to 15,000. The yen reverted to its former role as the niche currency of a single country. The 1990s became Japan's "lost decade," an era of economic stagnation and cultural ennui that left Americans and other non-Japanese wondering why they had ever feared the land of the rising sun.

The land of the dollar meanwhile rebounded. The end of the Cold War—whether marked by the 1989 breach of the Berlin Wall, the 1990 reunification of Germany or the 1991 demise of the Soviet Union—gave Americans cause for self-congratulation. Their system of democratic capitalism had finally bested the communist system of the Russians. Most Americans felt relieved; many felt triumphal. Nearly all began counting their country's "peace dividend": the dollars that would not be spent arming to defeat the suddenly defunct Soviet empire.

While all this was happening, George Bush made himself a fiscal liar. The Republican faithful had loved Ronald Reagan, and most were willing to accept as their hero's successor the man who had served as his vice president. But many harbored doubts that Bush was as committed to the conservative gospel as Reagan had been. Bush reassured them in the strongest language he could muster. "I'm the one who won't raise taxes," he told the 1988 Republican national convention. "My opponent [Democrat Michael Dukakis] now says he'll raise them as a last resort, or a third resort. When a politician talks like that, you know that's one resort he'll be checking into. My opponent won't rule out raising taxes. But I will. The Congress will push me to raise taxes, and I'll say no, and they'll push, and I'll say no, and they'll push again, and I'll say to them, 'Read my lips: no new taxes.'"

The convention bellowed its approval of this paraphrase of Clint Eastwood's tough-guy film character Dirty Harry. Bush, never known for his macho image, reveled in his Hollywood moment. But the moment passed, and after his election he confronted the reality of staggering federal deficits. The $25 billion shortfall that had shocked the markets in the 1960s had ballooned to more than $200 billion under Reagan. Tax cuts and new spending seemed to have knocked the federal budget forever beyond balance; the prospect spooked dollar-holders who once again fretted that Washington would have no choice but to inflate its way out of its hole. Purchasers of treasury bonds insisted on higher interest to hedge against inflation; the higher rates increased the deficit the more. The deficit became a drag on the larger economy, and the country slipped into recession.

Bush proposed a solution by cuts to federal spending. The Democrats who controlled Congress didn't rule out reductions on the spending side, but they insisted on increases on the revenue side. Bush dodged and weaved before accepting a compromise that included some modest tax increases.

The bargain cost him dearly. Party zealots screamed sellout; comedian David Letterman mocked Bush, saying: "Read my lips: I lied." The anger and ridicule weakened Bush for the 1992 election, prompting Texas billionaire H. Ross Perot to enter the presidential race.

But the bargain was the best thing to happen to the dollar in decades. It put the federal budget on track toward balance, a condition many observers had thought politically impossible. It heartened investors and producers sufficiently to lift the country out of the recession—although not soon enough to rescue Bush, who lost to Bill Clinton in the 1992 election.

Clinton's campaign team had kept its focus by reciting, "It's the economy, stupid," and when the economy rebounded, the new president reaped the benefits of Bush's budget compromise. The 1990s turned out to be the best decade for the economy since World War II. Employment, average income, profits and share prices all grew handsomely. After twenty years of inflation, recession and soaring deficits, the economy appeared back on track once more.

Share prices grew the fastest. The Dow did better than at any time since the 1920s—so well, in fact, as to defy explanation. "Even rising productivity could not explain the looniness of stock prices," Alan Greenspan recalled. The Fed chairman made a fetish of productivity, the metric that might have explained the booming stock market had the statistics shown that Americans were pumping out many more goods and services per hour. But the statistics did not show that, prompting Greenspan to conclude that the statistics must be wrong. Yet they weren't *that* wrong, and the rocketing share prices must have some other cause. "I had ongoing conversations with Bob Rubin on the subject," Greenspan said, referring to the treasury secretary. "We were both somewhat concerned. We'd now seen the Dow break through three 'millennium' marks— 4,000, 5,000, and 6,000—in just over a year and a half. Though economic growth was strong, we worried that investors were getting carried away." Greenspan thought a stock bubble was forming, as in the 1920s, and that when it burst it might flatten the whole economy, as in the 1930s. Greenspan's problem was to ease the air out of the bubble without bursting it.

"The concept of irrational exuberance came to me in the

bathtub one morning as I was writing a speech," he remembered. "The bathtub is where I get many of my best ideas. My
assistants have gotten used to typing from drafts scrawled on
damp yellow pads—a chore that got much easier once we found
a kind of pen whose ink doesn't run. Immersed in my bath, I'm
as happy as Archimedes as I contemplate the world."

Greenspan exhibited greater decorum than Archimedes,
who had leapt naked from his tub to share the concept of buoy-
ancy that later bore his name. The Fed chairman settled for
revealing his idea at the annual dinner of the American Enterprise Institute in the autumn of 1996. A hundred years after
the epic battle between Bryan and McKinley over silver and
gold, Greenspan reflected on the dollar's history since then. He
briefly recounted the creation of the Federal Reserve and the
evolution of its powers. He noted the deflation that had vexed
the American economy during the Great Depression, and he
observed that deflation's opposite—inflation—hadn't become a
concern until the 1960s. Within another decade inflation and
its pernicious consequences had compelled a shift in thinking
at the Fed. "The stagflation of the 1970s required a thorough
conceptual overhaul of economic thinking and policymaking,"
Greenspan said. Since then the Fed had focused on containing
inflation and the mindset it engendered. Greenspan forecast
more of the same. "The Congress willing, we will remain as the
guardian of the purchasing power of the dollar."

But guarding the dollar was easier to promise than to
accomplish, Greenspan said. The shift from an industrial economy to one based on services made merely defining the price
level, let alone preserving it, extremely difficult. "The price of
a ton of cold rolled steel sheet, or a linear yard of cotton broad
woven fabrics, could be reasonably compared over a period of
years." Services didn't compute or compare so easily. "What is
the price of a unit of software or a legal opinion? How does one
evaluate the price change of a cataract operation over a ten-
year period when the nature of the procedure and its impact on
the patient change so radically?" How broadly should the Fed

monitor prices? "Where do we draw the line on what prices matter? Certainly prices of goods and services now being produced. . . . But what about futures prices, or more importantly prices of claims on future goods and services, like equities, real estate, or other earning assets? Is stability of these prices essential to the stability of the economy?"

Greenspan offered no firm answers, only additional questions. Yet these questions appeared to connote answers toward which he, and presumably the Fed, were moving. "How do we know when irrational exuberance has unduly escalated asset values, which then become subject to unexpected and prolonged contractions? . . . How do we factor that assessment into monetary policy?"

Greenspan had a reputation for circumlocutive mumbling; his "irrational exuberance" phrasing amounted, for him, to a shout from the rooftops that stocks were overpriced. The obvious implication was that the Fed would tighten credit. Wall Street responded with a nosedive the next morning. But then the traders regained their confidence—or exuberance. "And the bull charged on," Greenspan remarked years later, still shaking his head.

In fact the bull gained roaring, snorting momentum. Previous bursts of technological innovation had prompted outbreaks of speculation: steam and railroads in the 1860s and 1870s, electricity in the 1920s. The Internet had the same effect in the 1990s. Even as the computer engineers, programmers and systems analysts built a virtual world out of zeroes and ones, the speculators, bankers and stock brokers built pyramids of virtual profits—airy predictions that nonetheless pulled in billions of real dollars. The market valued Amazon.com at $25 billion years before it made a nickel; eBay's shares tripled in price on the day of the company's initial public offering, without a profit in sight. The dot-com boom centered in Silicon Valley, where one venture capitalist described the "vein of gold" that ran through the area. "Anybody can reach down into it and strike it rich," he said. Another investor called the Internet boom "the largest legal creation of wealth in the history of the planet."

The dot-com boom sent the NASDAQ composite index, the most commonly cited measure of technology share prices, to unheard-of—undreamed-of—levels. The index quintupled in value between 1995 and 2000. The boom made millionaires of tens of thousands of employees of computer, software and Internet firms who took their pay in shares. Some let their windfalls ride; others cashed out and spent their money on real estate, creating a secondary surge in property values.

The good times lasted until March 2000, when the dot-com bubble burst with a violence that shocked even those who knew the tech stocks were overpriced. The NASDAQ dove 10 percent in a week, then another 20 percent. It kept plunging; by the end of the year it had given up half, obliterating trillions of dollars in market valuation.

By then George W. Bush had been elected president, after a disputed contest that sent additional shudders through the markets. Bush entered office committed to reducing the footprint of the federal government, and as a down payment he promised to trim taxes. "We will reduce taxes to recover the momentum of our economy and reward the effort and enterprise of working Americans," he declared in his inaugural address. The bulk of the benefit would go to those at the upper end of the income scale, where Bush proposed to cut the marginal rate from 40 percent to 33 percent. "I believe it's an important principle that no American should pay more than a third of his or her income to the federal government in federal taxes."

Bush got almost what he asked for on taxes; what he did *not* get were corresponding reductions in federal spending. Part of this was his fault: he knew, or must have known, that Congress always cuts taxes far more easily than it cuts spending. Cutting taxes induces pleasure in constituents; cutting spending causes pain. Bush's Republicans proved as averse to constituent pain as members of Congress typically have been; before long they were *increasing* spending, on all manner of worthy and dubious programs.

But some of Bush's failure to control the deficit resulted from events he didn't foresee. Whether he should have foreseen them was a question that evoked hot controversy during subsequent months and years. Either way, the terrorist attacks on New York and Washington on September 11, 2001, besides closing the stock exchange, jolting the financial system and casting a pall of anxiety across America, prompted the government to increase federal spending rather than reduce it. Congress and Bush approved a bailout of America's airlines, which had been struggling before September 11 and which, during the months after the attacks, could do little but watch as frightened passengers stayed home. The government strengthened security at airports and launched a war against Afghanistan, the training ground of al-Qaeda, the group responsible for the attacks. Two years later it launched a second war, against Saddam Hussein's Iraq.

The bill for the unanticipated spending came due as the tax cuts kicked in. The result was a stunning reversal of the progress that had been made against the federal debt under Clinton. The deficit mounted to nearly $600 billion per year, pushing the federal debt from 57 percent of GDP at the beginning of Bush's presidency to 70 percent by his last year in office.

The September 11 attacks made Americans realize they were vulnerable in ways they never had been before, and the realization came with a sobering corollary, that the very success of their system—symbolized most succinctly by the dollar—was what made them so vulnerable. The targeting of the World Trade Center by the suicide hijackers was no accident. The trade center, located in the heart of America's financial district, was the proudly thrusting symbol of the dollar's global reach. The center had been attacked before—in 1993, when a truck bomber blew up a vehicle in the underground garage. The explosion rocked the building, killing several people and wounding hundreds. The 2001 strikes, which killed thousands and brought the twin towers down, finished the job.

There was something else about the attacks that linked them to the dollar. Though airplanes were the proximate weapon, the dollar was what made the attacks possible. Osama bin Laden became the guiding spirit of al-Qaeda not only because he was charismatic but because he was rich. Family money—petrodollars, indirectly—allowed him to indulge his militant interpretation of Islam and to fund the terrorist army he gathered around him. The ubiquity of the dollar—its universal acceptance on markets legal and illegal—enabled al-Qaeda to acquire the equipment and training to carry out the attacks Osama and his followers hoped would restore Islam to the purity and primacy they deemed its due.

The American government understood the role of the dollar in facilitating terrorism. Bush immediately froze the assets of dozens of groups suspected of aiding terrorists. "Today we have launched a strike on the financial foundation of the global terror network," he said. "We will starve the terrorists of funding." He called on other governments to join the effort. "Money is the life-blood of terrorist operations. Today we're asking the world to stop payment." Congress didn't wait for allies. The legislature approved the USA Patriot Act, which granted executive and law enforcement agencies—including the Federal Reserve—sweeping powers to move against individuals, associations and banks suspected of involvement in terrorist activities.

As the war on terror escalated, so did efforts to interdict dollars bound for terrorists. "For years, individuals and charities based in Saudi Arabia have been the most important source of funds for Al-Qaeda," a task force convened by the Council on Foreign Relations asserted. "And for years, Saudi officials have turned a blind eye to this problem." The task force, a phalanx of former diplomats, treasury and Fed officials and intelligence and law-enforcement officers, urged the Bush administration to compel Saudi cooperation. "As long as Al-Qaeda retains access to a viable financial network, it remains a lethal threat to the United States." The administration did pressure the Saudis, although with less rigor than it doubtless would have employed had the Saudis lacked oil. It also levied sanctions against countries it publicly identified as underwriters of terrorism, including Iran, Libya and North Korea.

The targets of the interdiction efforts responded with measures that might have been considered enterprising in another context. The Taliban of Afghanistan, after being driven from power in Kabul, took control of the country's drug business. American sources estimated that the Taliban reaped as much as $300 million per year from opium. "Opium is their financial engine," an American general stated. American forces raiding Taliban strongholds found opium and weapons intermingled. "We often come across a compound that has opium and I.E.D. [improvised explosive device] materials side by side, and opium and explosive materials and weapons. It's very common." American troops tried to halt the trade, without lasting effect. A reporter and an interpreter accompanied soldiers among fields of opium poppies. "I'm very happy to see you," a farmer told the troops, through the interpreter. "Really?" one of the Americans replied. "Yes," the farmer said. The interpreter turned to the American and said in English: "He's a liar."

"We're All Americans Now," *Le Monde* of Paris had headlined after the September 11 terrorist attacks, which evoked a foreign wave of pro-American sympathy unlike anything seen since 1945. The sympathy extended to support for the war against al-Qaeda in Afghanistan, with the British accompanying the Americans at once, and other NATO members joining later.

But the sympathy did not cause Europe to delay the launch of the most serious competitor to the dollar since the decline of the British pound decades earlier. The European Economic Community had expanded during the 1970s to embrace Britain, Ireland and Denmark, in addition to the founding six. The old and new members pondered a single currency, one that would obviate the money-changing that made cross-border transactions inefficient even in the absence of tariff barriers. To lay the groundwork, the members established an exchange-rate mechanism that strictly limited the fluctuation of one currency against the others.

Further integration followed. In 1979 elections to a European parliament were held. The Schengen agreement of 1985 eliminated passport controls at border crossings. The collapse of the Soviet alliance system in the late 1980s allowed the expansion of the European Community to the east. The Maastricht treaty of 1992 rechristened the organization as the European Union and confirmed the "four freedoms" of the single European market: the free movement of goods, services, people and money. Planning for the new currency proceeded apace, and in January 1999 the euro was launched, albeit, at this point, as merely an electronic currency of account.

The physical introduction of euro notes and coins at the beginning of 2002 was fraught with uncertainty. The proponents of the single-Europe project hailed the arrival and conspicuously fitted the euro into their daily lives. The finance minister of Belgium led reporters to a cash machine near European Union headquarters in Brussels and withdrew 150 euros in crisp notes. "I'm going to start by buying myself a Belgian beer," he announced with a smile. Reactions elsewhere were mixed. "The old notes are beautiful; the new notes are ugly," a fruit seller in Paris opined. Italy's minister for institutional reform didn't appreciate this reform at all. "I couldn't care less about the euro," he said. "This was a decision imposed from on high and the public had no choice in the matter." A French trade-union leader, remarking that the French government and French business had staked their prestige on the success of the euro, promised to put the euro to good, if unintended, use. "A golden opportunity like this is unlikely to come our way again," he said. "Our employers are in a position where they must negotiate, and, if necessary, we will hit them where it hurts."

Americans were underwhelmed by the advent of the dollar's new competitor. "Euro's Debut Has Little Impact on Us, for Now," the *Wall Street Journal* headlined. A Manhattan currency trader commented: "Things went very well for the conversion but I don't think it is anything more than a honeymoon for the euro."

The honeymoon was pleasant if not breathtakingly passionate. After opening a bit below $1.20 per euro in 1999 the euro had slid to less than 90 cents. The introduction of notes and coins inspired confidence among consumers and investors, and by the end of the summer of 2002 it had returned to parity with the dollar: 1 dollar per 1 euro.

The introduction of the euro notes inspired the U.S. government to revamp the American currency. In June 2002 the treasury and the Federal Reserve jointly announced a redesign of America's notes. "The purpose of the currency redesign is to stay ahead of advanced computer technologies used for some types of counterfeiting," the announcement said. It went on to report that the Secret Service reckoned that $47 million in false currency had entered circulation during the previous year alone. The new bills would retain such existing security measures as watermarks visible under ordinary light, special threads woven into the paper that became apparent only under ultraviolet light, microprinting that was difficult to reproduce and ink that shifted shade when the angle of vision changed. New measures would center on subtle colors added to the background, making the bills difficult to photocopy convincingly.

The redesign would commence with the three largest bills: $100, $50 and $20. The $10 and $5 notes would follow. "A redesign of the $2 and $1 notes is not included in the plans," the announcement said tersely. Some Americans might have been surprised at the reminder that $2 notes even existed, so infrequently did they circulate; as for the $1 bill, it was such small change that counterfeiters didn't bother faking it. Besides, treasury officials hoped to wean Americans from the dollar bill in favor of dollar coins, which lasted far longer.

A certain class of persons took special interest in the redesign of the $100 bill. The note, featuring a portrait of Benjamin Franklin, appeared infrequently in the wallets and purses of law-abiding citizens, most of whom used checks or credit cards for transactions of more than fifty or sixty dollars. But it was the favored currency on the black markets of the world and in shady dealings generally. A thousand dollars in hundreds fit easily in an envelope, a million dollars in a suitcase. "Benjamins" were universally recognized and accepted; it was estimated that if the notes were to disappear, a great deal of the world's crime would skid to a halt, at least briefly. For this reason, recommendations to recall the hundred were a regular feature of law enforcement life. Honest citizens with at most handfuls of the notes wouldn't be embarrassed to redeem them; criminals with satchels-full would be stuck with worthless paper.

But the hundred earned the government too much money to be abandoned. A single note cost six cents to produce but was sold to banks for its face value (in the case of new issues; replacement of worn-out bills was a break-even affair). The difference, called "seigniorage," amounted to billions of dollars each year, which the treasury was loath to surrender. Other notes produced profits, too, but for none of them was the margin so wide. (Small coins suffered negative seigniorage, being more expensive to produce than they were worth, which was why the treasury tried, unsuccessfully, to discontinue the penny.)

The American hundred became a mainstay of some foreign economies. During the Cold War the bill had circulated surreptitiously in the countries of the Soviet bloc; after the collapse of communism it openly replaced the discredited currency of discredited regimes. An American reporter in Moscow in the mid-1990s described the importance of the American currency. "If there's anywhere in the world where the dollar is still almighty, it's Russia," he wrote. This reporter had studied the question carefully and compiled some rough figures. "More than $100 million comes into the country each day, and there is something on the order of $20 billion in greenbacks in circulation, more than in any country outside the United States itself. That comes to $400 for every family in Russia, probably as much or more than the value of Russian rubles in circulation. And 80 percent of it is in $100 bills. Urban grandmothers save C-notes to safeguard their retirements. Slick New Russians in Moscow peel them from fat wads to pay for dinner, a sports car or a new dacha in the country. Mafia dons carry U.S. hundreds around in attaché cases. And whoever can manage to be paid his salary in dollars, does."

An earlier redesign of the hundred had put many Russians on edge. "People are all stirred up," a Moscow banker declared. "They're calling like crazy." Russians had a bad history with their own currency, which was periodically recalled and devalued; in the previous three years the ruble had lost 80 percent of its purchasing power. Hence the flight to the dollar, and hence panic at the thought that the stashes of American hundreds were in danger. The American ambassador in Moscow took the extraordinary step of issuing a statement on behalf of his country's currency, despite the fact that the dollar was technically illegal for retail purchases in Russia. "The notes that you currently have will still remain valid and will still be honored by the United States government at their full face value," Thomas Pickering promised. Not all Russians were convinced. "People have been deceived so many times during these barbaric exchange campaigns that psychologically they will expect some sort of dirty trick on the part of the state or banks," a publishing executive who declined to give his name declared. Yet the Russians weren't about to trade in their dollars for rubles. "If you want to save money or take a vacation or buy something important, dollars are safer and better," a salesman who traveled often to Western Europe explained.

The appearance of the euro foretold new competition for the dollar in such nervous currency markets as Russia. International law enforcement officials complained openly of something America's treasury men muttered quietly about: that the largest euro bill, of five hundred euros, might displace the American hundred as criminals' currency of choice. For the T-men the issue was the loss of seigniorage; for the lawmen the problem was the punch the big euro bill carried. The suitcase required to hold a million dollars in American hundreds could be replaced by a handbag of the euro notes, making transport easier and harder to stop.

But for the moment the crooks appeared to be sticking with their $100 bills. The point of dealing in cash was to avoid attracting attention; until the novelty of the euros wore off, the American Benjamins were a safer bet.

≡ BE NICE TO YOUR CREDITORS ≡
2003—

"It's China's World. We Just Live in It," *Fortune* announced in October 2009. The accompanying article described a prospecting trip in Africa by officials of the China National Offshore Oil Corporation. Nigeria was renewing production licenses in its oil fields, and CNOOC was aiming to elbow aside such traditional players as Exxon Mobil and Royal Dutch Shell. "The Beijing-based company wants to secure no less than one-sixth of the African nation's production," the article asserted. "And CNOOC, apparently, isn't screwing around." China's sudden appearance distressed the existing licensees but delighted the Nigerians. "We love this kind of competition," a spokesman for the government said.

The *Fortune* piece went on to describe other properties the Chinese were snapping up. Just the previous month the China Investment Corporation, the government's sovereign wealth fund, had spent a billion dollars on a minority stake in a Kazakhstan oil and gas company. About the same time the CIC paid $850 million for part of a Hong Kong trading firm. The China Development Bank floated Brazil a $10 billion loan to underwrite exploration off the South American coast. "So far this decade," the *Fortune* correspondent recounted breathlessly, "China has spent an estimated $115 billion on foreign acquisitions. Now that the nation is sitting on massive foreign-exchange wealth ($2.1 trillion and counting), it is eager to find something (anything!) to invest in besides U.S. Treasury debt."

Alan Greenspan had something to do with China's eagerness to escape the dollar. The September 11 terrorist attacks, coming on the heels of the dot-com crash, had frightened investors; to forestall a recession the Fed cut interest rates, and when this didn't provide a sufficient boost, it cut them again—and again and again. By mid-2003 the federal funds rate touched 1 percent, from a recent high of 6.5 percent. Investors remained leery of stocks, but they found real estate attractive at the low interest rates. Money poured into land and buildings, which seemed eminently more substantial than the recently busted empires of the ether. Prices shot up, doubling and tripling in certain markets in just a few years. As in most bubbles, self-conscious speculators were joined by persons who sincerely believed in the permanence of this trend. After all, the supply of land was limited, by no less an authority than God, while population continued to grow. And as in previous bubbles, rules and practices designed to deter excessive speculation were bent or ignored. Lenders loosened standards for determining who got mortgages; "subprime" packages seemed reasonable on the premise that prices would continue to climb, allowing borrowers to remedy any weaknesses in their résumés or credit histories. Adjustable-rate mortgages let buyers postpone paying the full cost of their loans, again on the assumption of rising prices, which would allow refinancing or sale before the higher rates kicked in. Lenders were happy to make the loans, as they collected origination fees and then sold the loans to other institutions. The risk was mitigated by the bundling of many loans into large packages; a few loans might fail, but the profits on the good loans would more than compensate for the losses on the bad.

Or so what passed for conventional wisdom contended. Whether it was really wisdom was hard to tell, for the bundled

loans were merely one class of a large variety of novel financial instruments that often seemed mystifying even to those
who invented them. Generically called "derivatives," the new
instruments had roots in the desire of investors to hedge their
bets. Credit-default swaps, for example, allowed the purchasers of risky bonds to reduce the risk by what amounted to
insurance policies. A bondholder would pay a third party a
small amount of money as a premium; if the bond failed, the
third party would cover the loss. On a rising market, everyone
gained. The third parties collected many premiums and covered few losses; the bondholders slept soundly.

Occasional skeptics pointed out that this insurance wasn't
like other insurance. What rendered auto insurance and life
insurance actuarially robust was that policyholders' risks
were independent. Jones's car wreck didn't make a collision
for Smith any more likely; Garza's cancer didn't increase the
stroke danger to Lee. But holders of mortgages and other bonds
were linked. If the price of one property fell, the prices of others were likely to slide too. The bankruptcy of one corporation
might well destabilize others.

The precise cause of the panic of 2008 was as hard to iden-
tify as the triggers of most panics. Real estate prices hesitated
in their run-up and in doing so gave pause to speculators and
their lenders. A run on the British bank Northern Rock boded
ill for similarly extended institutions in Europe and the United
States. The American firm Bear Stearns stumbled and had to
seek shelter in a merger with J. P. Morgan Chase (itself the
result of an earlier merger between J. P. Morgan's eponymous
company and David Rockefeller's Chase Manhattan Bank).

Suddenly everything seemed at risk. The optimism that had
inflated the real estate bubble vanished, precipitating a fall in
prices. The falling prices put lenders at risk, including many
who had purchased the bundles of mortgages without fully
realizing what they had gotten into. The interconnections that
characterized the modern financial system, and which had
engendered confidence while prices were rising, now deep-

ened the panic as the wobbly firms threatened to bring down the entire system.

The panic elected Barack Obama, who had trailed Republican war hero John McCain while the country's concerns centered on the wars in Iraq and Afghanistan, but who erased the gap after the economy shuddered. The panic meanwhile tested Ben Bernanke's understanding of history and his willingness to apply the lessons of the past to the present. Bernanke, as a Princeton professor of economics, had drawn attention with an opinion piece in the *Wall Street Journal* in which he asked, "What happens when Greenspan is gone?" The answer he gave—"The Fed needs an approach that consolidates the gains of the Greenspan years and ensures that those successful policies will continue, even if future Fed chairmen are less skillful or less committed to price stability than Mr. Greenspan has been"—satisfied George W. Bush, who tapped Bernanke to succeed Greenspan.

Bernanke had studied the Great Depression in detail and concluded that the Fed had fatally erred in letting the money supply shrink as drastically as it did. He insisted that such a failure not be repeated. In a widely noted address to the National Economists Club, titled "Deflation: Making Sure It Doesn't Happen Here," he pointed to the stagnant Japanese economy as showing how deflation could sap the most vibrant system. He suggested that American inflation had been tamed perhaps too well and that deflation was a real threat. But he also stated that it needn't occur. "The sources of deflation are not a mystery," he said. "Deflation is in almost all cases a side effect of a collapse of aggregate demand—a drop in spending so severe that producers must cut prices on an ongoing basis in order to find buyers." The prescription for preventing deflation was no mystery either. "Use monetary and fiscal policy as needed to support aggregate spending, in a manner as nearly consistent as possible with full utilization of economic resources and low and stable inflation." In a grave cri-

sis the Fed's ordinary tools of monetary policy might not suf-
fice; the board then should take stronger action. The Fed could
lend directly to troubled banks at low or zero rates of interest,
ensuring liquidity in the credit markets. If necessary the Fed,
in cooperation with the treasury, could manipulate the dollar's value against other currencies. "I need to tread carefully
here," Bernanke acknowledged. "Manipulating the exchange
value of the dollar would not be a particularly desirable way to
fight domestic deflation, particularly given the range of other
options available." But it could work. "A striking example from
U.S. history is Franklin Roosevelt's 40 percent devaluation of
the dollar against gold in 1933–34, enforced by a program of
gold purchases and domestic money creation. The devaluation
and the rapid increase in money supply it permitted ended
the U.S. deflation remarkably quickly. . . . The economy grew
strongly, and by the way, 1934 was one of the best years of the
century for the stock market."

Bernanke's boldness served him well in the autumn of 2008.
Falling home prices pushed the Federal National Mortgage
Association, commonly called Fannie Mae, and its cousin the
Federal Home Loan Mortgage Corporation, or Freddie Mac,
to the verge of dissolution; related problems similarly drove
the American International Group, or AIG, to the edge. The
Fed and the treasury had already furnished support to Fannie,
Freddie and AIG, but more appeared necessary. Meanwhile
Lehman Brothers, a big financial house, also teetered. Lehman
looked to the government for help, but Bernanke and treasury
secretary Henry Paulson declined to give it, on the reasoning
that Washington couldn't and shouldn't save every firm from
its folly. But Lehman's subsequent bankruptcy—the largest fil-
ing in American history—sent new shocks through the system.
The Dow Jones average plunged 500 points; nearly every bank
and financial house appeared in jeopardy. The next day a large
money market fund announced that it had "broken the buck"—
been forced to pay depositors less than a dollar for each dollar
of deposits. The Dow dropped another 450 points. "It felt like

there was no ground beneath your feet," one Wall Street veteran said. "I didn't know where it was going to end."

The chaos prompted Bernanke and Paulson to move decisively. They crafted a $700 billion bailout package for the financial sector and on Thursday evening, September 18, took it to Capitol Hill. In the conference room of House speaker Nancy Pelosi they huddled with the congressional leadership. "We are in danger of a broad systemic collapse," Paulson said. "Action needs to be taken urgently to head it off. We need the authority to spend several hundred billion dollars." Bernanke explained that he had devoted decades to examining the 1930s depression; the current situation looked alarmingly like that. "The kind of financial collapse we're now on the brink of is always followed by a long, deep recession," Bernanke said. "If we aren't able to head this off, the next generation of economists will be writing not about the 1930s but about this." Some of the legislators responded that a package as big as Bernanke and Paulson wanted would require time to pass. "You have no idea what you're asking me to do," Senate majority leader Harry Reid said. "It takes me forty-eight hours to get the Republicans to flush the toilet." Others accepted Bernanke's assessment of the danger. "That meeting was one of the most astounding experiences I've had in my thirty-four years in politics," Charles Schumer, a Democratic senator from New York, said. "When you listened to him describe it, you gulped." The Fed chief reemphasized his point. Without swift action the crisis could become a catastrophe, he said. "If we don't do this, we may not have an economy on Monday."

After the unnerved lawmakers signed on to Bernanke's package, George Bush took the case for a rescue to the American people. "Our system of free enterprise rests on the conviction that the federal government should interfere in the marketplace only when necessary," the president said. "Given the precarious state of today's financial markets, and their vital importance to the daily lives of the American people, government intervention is not only warranted, it is essential."

Bush described the measures already taken and those proposed, including purchase by the government of the troubled
assets of threatened financial firms. He closed on a note from
Franklin Roosevelt's fireside chat at the crucial moment of the
banking crisis of 1933. "America's financial system is intricate
and complex," Bush said. "But behind all the technical terminology and statistics is a critical human factor: confidence.
Confidence in our financial system and in its institutions is
essential to the smooth operation of our economy. . . . Investors should know that the United States government is taking
action to restore confidence in America's financial markets so
they can thrive again."

The rescue package stemmed the panic, and by the time
of Barack Obama's inauguration the worst was over. But
the broader recession the panic precipitated continued, and
indeed intensified far into 2009. The new administration and
the Democratic Congress approved an $800 billion economic
stimulus package, but the federal spending failed to halt the
rise in unemployment, which topped 10 percent by the autumn.
The most obvious effect of the stimulus was to swell the federal
deficit to a level inconceivable only a year earlier. The $1.4 tril-
lion gap was three times the previous year's deficit and more
than the total debt accumulated during the first two centuries
of America's national existence. Frighteningly credible esti-
mates forecast trillion-dollar deficits for at least a decade.

The red tide augured ill for the dollar, as foreign holders of
greenbacks weighed more seriously than ever ditching the
dollar for other currencies. Gao Xiqing, the head of the China
Investment Corporation, had studied the issue for years. Gao
was an improbable money man, being a card-carrying Communist and the son of a Red Army officer who had made the Long
March with Mao Zedong. But Gao had attended law school
in the United States, at Duke University, and had worked in
finance in New York after graduation. He thought more like a
capitalist than most Americans. Nor did he hesitate to lecture

Americans on how they had strayed from the capitalist road, as journalist James Fallows discovered. "Does America wonder who its new Chinese banking overlords might be?" Fallows asked *Atlantic Monthly* readers. "This is what one of the very most influential of them had to say about the world financial crisis, what is wrong with Wall Street, whether one still-poor country with tremendous internal needs could continue subsidizing a still-rich one, and how he thought America could adjust to its 'realistic' place in the world."

Gao told Fallows that Americans had lost the entrepreneurial spirit that had made their country great. "Americans started believing that they can live on other people's money," Gao said. "And more and more so. First other people's money in your own country. And then the savings rate comes down, and you start living on other people's money from outside. At first it was the Japanese. Now the Chinese and the Middle Easterners." The model was unsustainable. "We—the Chinese, the Middle Easterners, the Japanese—we can see this. . . . We'd love to support you guys—if it's sustainable. But if it's not, why should we be doing this? After we are gone, you cannot just go to the moon to get more money. So, forget it. Let's change the way of living."

The derivatives that underpinned the recent speculation on Wall Street revealed the hollowness of the current American approach to wealth creation, Gao said. "If you look at every one of these products, they make sense. But in aggregate, they are bullshit. They are crap. They serve to cheat people. I was predicting this many years ago." He told of a session with China's political leaders. "They wanted me to explain about capital markets and how they worked. These were all ministers and mostly not from a financial background. So I wondered, How do I explain derivatives? I used the model of mirrors. First of all, you have this book to sell." He picked up a book from his desk. "This is worth something, because of all the labor and so on you put in it. But then someone says, 'I don't have to sell the book itself! I have a mirror, and I can sell the mirror image of

116

the book!' Okay. That's a stock certificate. And then someone else says, 'I have another mirror—I can sell a mirror image of that mirror.' Derivatives. That's fine too, for a while. Then you have 10,000 mirrors, and the image is almost perfect. People start to believe that these mirrors are almost the real thing. But at some point, the image is interrupted. And all the rest will go. . . . This is what happened with the American economy, and it will be a long and painful process to come down."

Fallows asked if Gao or his associates had been consulted by the Americans as Bernanke and Paulson formulated their rescue of the financial system. "Not directly. We were talking to people there, and they were hoping that we would be supportive by not pulling out our money. We know that by pulling out money, we're not serving anyone's good, including ourselves. . . . So we're trying to help, at least by not aggravating the problem." But consultation would be necessary at some point. "At the end of the day, the American government needs to talk with people and say: 'Why don't we get together and think about this? If China has $2 trillion, Japan has almost $2 trillion, and Russia has some, and all the others, then let's throw away the ideological differences and think about what's good for everyone.' We can get all the relevant people together and think up what people are calling a second Bretton Woods system, like the first Bretton Woods convention did."

Fallows suggested that if China began withdrawing its dollar assets, it would hurt itself. "In the short term," Gao conceded. But the long term might be different. He explained the problems the Chinese government faced as a result of its continued investment in America. "We have a PR department, which collects all the comments about us, from Chinese newspapers and the Web. Every night, I try to pick a time when I'm in a relatively good mood to read it, because most of the comments are very critical of us. Recently we increased our holdings in Blackstone a little bit. Now we're increasing a little bit our holdings in Morgan Stanley, so as not to be diluted by the Japanese. People here [in China] hate it. They come out and say, 'Why the hell are you trying to save those people? You are the representative of the poor people eating porridge, and you're saving people eating shark fins!' It's always that sort of thing."

Fallows pointed out that many Americans distrusted China's intentions. Gao nodded. "I can understand why Americans might feel that way," he said. But the feeling had little to do with China itself. "It could be any country. It could be Japan, or Germany. This generation of Americans is so used to your supremacy. Your being treated nicely by everyone. It hurts to think, Okay, now we have to be on equal footing to other people. 'On equal footing' would necessarily mean that sometimes you have to stoop to appear to be humble to other people." Yet Americans would do well to learn humility. "The simple truth today is that your economy is built on the global economy. And it's built on the support, the gratuitous support, of a lot of countries. So why don't you come over and, I won't say kowtow"—here he laughed—"but at least, be *nice* to the countries that lend you money."

Sooner or later Americans would have to make deep changes in their overall approach to the world. "Pull your troops back! Take the troops back, demobilize many of the troops, so that you can save some money rather than spending $2 billion every day on them. And then tell your people that you need to save, and come out with a long-term, sustainable financial policy." The American government needed to speak frankly to the American people. "This is about the survival of our nation," it should say. "It's not about our supremacy in the world. Let's not even talk about that anymore. Let's get down to the very basics of our livelihood."

And if the American government wouldn't deliver the message, foreigners like Gao would. "I have great admiration of American people," he said. "Creative, hard-working, trusting, and freedom-loving. But you have to have someone to tell you the truth. And then, start realizing it. And if you do it, just like what you did in the Second World War, then you'll be great again! If that happens, then of course American power would still be there for at least as long as I am living. But many people are betting on the other side."

The nineteenth century had been the era of the gold standard, the twentieth of the dollar standard. What the twenty-first century would be was anyone's guess. But some guesses were more credible than others. The dollar had had a good run. It made America rich; it saved democracy; it defeated communism. Yet it suffered from its very success. As the closest thing to a world currency, it knitted the planet into a single economy more fully than any currency before. In doing so it spread prosperity more widely than prosperity had ever been spread, but it diluted prosperity for those—steelworkers in America, maize farmers in Mexico, cobblers in Italy—who found they couldn't compete in the new world market.

And it magnified the effects of the instabilities that have always afflicted dynamic markets. The financial panics of the early nineteenth century in America were local affairs, confined to a modest number of firms and affecting comparatively few people. The panics of the late nineteenth century had national effects, with some transatlantic connections via the gold standard, yet most of the world hardly noticed. In the modern era—the era of the dollar—the world couldn't help noticing. The panic of 1929 helped trigger the global crisis of the 1930s. Not by accident did the nations of the world, gathered in London in 1933, listen for Franklin Roosevelt to declare the value of the dollar and thereby decree their fate. Richard Nixon's closing of the gold window in 1971 rocked financial markets from London to Tokyo and Buenos Aires to Bombay. The dot-com bubble of the late 1990s burst in Silicon Valley but blew out lights in Bangalore and Mumbai (Bombay's new name), Shanghai and Taipei, Seoul and Sydney.

And then things got really hairy. The first years of the new century witnessed risk-taking on a scale never experienced before and hardly ever imagined. Wall Street leveraged debt in real estate, in corporate shares, in derivatives, in a hundred other instruments that paid dizzying returns when the markets smiled—and exacted harrowing revenge when the markets growled. Foreign firms, big and small, joined the action; the tiny country of Iceland became a banking powerhouse and the richest nation in the world on a per capita basis—until the financial markets crashed and left the country staggering under a debt equivalent to seven times its total annual production. The Persian Gulf city-state of Dubai commenced a building program that would have made the Egyptian pharaohs weep tears of envy down their pyramids, until the bill came due and the government said it might have to default on $60 billion of loans. Half a world away the Dow dropped 200 points on the news; Asian markets plunged even more.

The global connections amplified the effects of the casino economy in America, corroding the social compact on which the dollar's domestic success had been based. Ordinary Americans had rarely begrudged the wealth of the few, partly because they believed the wealth was fairly earned and partly because they hoped they or their children might become wealthy someday. But the compact weakened when corporate executives took home tens of millions of dollars a year even as workers' pay stagnated, and it nearly failed when those same workers found themselves, through their tax dollars, cleaning up the mess the executives had created and guaranteeing, in many cases, the fat cats' exorbitant compensation.

The anger spilled over against the Fed, the institution that had done more than any other to manage the dollar's dominion. "Ben S. Bernanke doesn't know how lucky he is," financial writer James Grant said. "Tongue-lashings from Bernie Sanders, the populist senator from Vermont, are one thing. The hangman's noose is another." Grant explained that the Coinage Act of 1792 mandated the death penalty for any public official who fraudulently debased the dollar; Sanders and others blamed Bernanke for debasing the dollar by letting the casino economy spin out of control. "For many years I held the Federal Reserve in very high regard," Richard Shelby, the ranking Republican on the Senate banking committee, said. "I fear now, however, that our trust and confidence were misplaced." Bernanke was summoned to Congress and made to plead contrition. "There were mistakes made all around," the Fed chief acknowledged. "I did not anticipate a crisis of this magnitude and this severity. We should have required more capital, more liquidity. We should have required more risk-management controls."

Bernanke's mea culpas saved his job; he was appointed to a second term as Fed chief. But they did nothing to ease the strain on the dollar. America was caught on the horns of a dilemma: reducing the deficit in the short term required raising taxes, but raising taxes risked stifling a recovery and aggravating the deficit in the long term. "Doing the prudent thing about deficits now would be an extremely foolish thing," economist Paul Krugman observed.

The problem appeared intractable. James Grant proclaimed a "Requiem for the Dollar" in the *Wall Street Journal*. "The dollar is faith-based," Grant said. "There's nothing behind it but Congress. And now the world is losing faith, as well it might." The dollar's good years were all in the past. "The greenback is a glorious old brand that's looking more and more like General Motors."

The dollar's demise, if it came to that, would be America's problem, but the world's as well. Much of the planet had come to depend on the dollar, and replacing it would be difficult and painful. No alternative reserve currency made a compelling claim. Use of the euro was spreading, but the EU's money lacked the ubiquity of the greenback, and efforts to rescue the Greek government in 2010 revealed deep rifts in the euro zone. China's currency, the yuan, wasn't even traded on world markets. Japan's once-mighty yen still floundered two decades after Tokyo's swoon. Besides, with so much of the world invested in the dollar, the costs of changing over to another root currency would be prohibitive.

But the alternative to the dollar need not be a single currency. When Gao Xiqing and others spoke of a second Bretton Woods conference, they envisioned replacing the dollar with a market basket of moneys. No one of the currencies need be as strong as the dollar had been; together they could do what the dollar no longer could. The market basket approach had its own problems, but as time passed and the American deficit continued to grow, the dollar doubters seemed ever more likely to have their way. Financial power talked, just as it had for the Americans at the first Bretton Woods conference.

A postdollar world would look different than what Americans were used to. The American economy couldn't help but suffer, at least comparatively. The strength of the American economy had made the dollar's hegemony possible, but the dollar's hegemony had preserved and extended the economy's strength. Americans could devalue the dollar and thereby transfer costs of domestic reform to the rest of the world, as Franklin Roosevelt demonstrated in the 1930s. Americans could have guns and butter despite an imbalance of international payments, as Lyndon Johnson showed in the 1960s. Americans could export inflation and cushion themselves against oil price rises, as Richard Nixon and his successors revealed in the 1970s. In a postdollar world such finesses and acts of force majeure would be far more difficult; the American economy would have to stand more solidly on its own footing.

By 2010 the decline of the dollar was already limiting America's freedom of action. The debate over health care reform during Barack Obama's first year turned as much on what the competing proposals would do to the federal deficit as on what they implied for patients and doctors. The cost of the wars in Iraq and Afghanistan, which passed a trillion dollars in 2010, effectively ruled out additional elective wars, almost regardless of the provocation. Ben Bernanke and the Fed didn't take a step without considering how the Chinese and other big creditors would respond.

In a postdollar world Americans would learn to get by with

less. The consumer binge of the 1990s and early 2000s had been financed by foreign lending; as foreign lenders diversified their portfolios Americans would be compelled to live within their incomes again. The adjustment threatened to be traumatic; the newly enforced thrift was translating into unemployment in the consumer sector, recently a pillar of the American economy. The layoffs wouldn't be temporary, but structural; the superfluous sales clerks, shelf fillers and advertising executives would have to retool for other work. In the economy of thrift, real estate values would take years or decades to return to their prebust levels. Builders reported that the McMansion, the trophy home of the boom years, was giving way to a downsized model of the American dream.

Americans would have to take collective actions they had previously avoided. With bondholders balking at larger deficits, Americans would have to balance the books of Social Security and Medicare. They would have to stay in the workforce longer and accept smaller pensions. The elderly would have to pay more for health care and would receive less of it. A political war of generations could develop as Americans remembered that Social Security and Medicare transferred money from the young to the old.

On the other hand, perhaps the dollar's run wasn't finished. Indeed, by making the changes the dollar's decline would force on them, Americans would increase the greenback's chances of remaining the planet's reserve currency. Whether this would be a good thing—for America or for the planet—wasn't obvious. The dollar era had been a time of global growth, but of global fragility as well. Perhaps the growth was possible without the fragility; perhaps a new generation of financial leaders would discover how to keep booms from becoming busts; perhaps fresh minds could halt ambition short of hubris.

Perhaps.

≡ NOTES ≡

1. *Fiat Lucre:* 1863–1907

4 "to coin money": Article 1, section 8, U.S. Constitution.

4–5 "Dollars or units": *Statutes at Large*, Second Congress, session 1, chapter 16 (April 2, 1792), 248.

7 "When the laws": Jackson veto message, July 10, 1832, Public Papers of the Presidents, American Presidency Project, http://www.presidency.ucsb.edu/ws/index.php?pid=67043 (accessed August 19, 2010).

7 "The Bank, Mr. Van Buren": H. W. Brands, *Andrew Jackson* (2005), 500.

10 "To make these notes legal tender": *Congressional Globe,* 37th Congress, 2nd session, 682.

10–11 "I would admit the plea of necessity": Ibid., 691.

11 "I have felt": Ibid., 618.

11–12 "The bill before us": Ibid., 523.

12 "Surely we must all be": Ibid., 799–800.

12 "lawful money and a legal tender": *Statutes at Large*, 37th Congress, 2nd session, 12:345.

12 "Thereafter the right": Ibid., 12:711.

13 129 greenback dollars were required to purchase 100 gold dollars: Wesley Clair Mitchell, *A History of the Greenbacks, With Special Reference to the Economic Consequences of Their Issue, 1862–65* (1903), 245.

13   "Along with ordinary happenings": Maury Klein, *The Life and Legend of Jay Gould* (1986), 69.

13   "Imagine a rat-pit in full blast": Horace White, *Money and Banking, Illustrated by American History* (1896), 176–177.

14   "The bear party at times . . . involved in ruin": H. W. Brands, *The Money Men* (2006), 151–157.

16   "It is certainly not the same power": *Hepburn v. Griswold*, 75 U.S. 603.

18–19   "I have come down to Washington . . . goal has been reached": Brands, *Money Men*, 177–179.

20   "Some men are so ugly . . . a cross of gold!'": "William Jennings Bryan," *Review of Reviews*, August 15, 1896, 124–127.

22   "The dollar consisting of twenty-five and eight-tenths grains of gold": Gold Standard Act, March 14, 1900, 31 Stat. 45.

23   "Mr. Morgan could not be waked up . . . here's the pen": Frederick Lewis Allen, "Morgan the Great," *Life*, April 25, 1949, 123ff.

2. *Strong and Stronger*: 1907–1928

26–27   "You are an advocate of combination . . . all the bonds in Christendom": *New York Times*, December 20, 1912.

30   "And to think": Ron Chernow, *The House of Morgan* (1990), 159.

30   "great and rapidly growing concentration": *Report of the Committee Appointed Pursuant to House Resolutions 429 and 504 to Investigate the Concentration of Control of Money and Credit* (1913), 129, 140.

31   "I remember giving Mr. Whitson": Lester V. Chandler, *Benjamin Strong* (1958), 29.

32   "fatally defective . . . suggestion of compromise": Ibid., 34–37.

32–33   "The said notes shall be obligations": Federal Reserve Act, December 23, 1913, 35 Stat. 251.

33   "We have created a democracy of credit": H. W. Brands, *Woodrow Wilson* (2003), 38.

33   "We must all bend our energies": Chandler, *Benjamin Strong*, 37.

34   "The principles of a central bank . . . relating to the System": Ibid., 39–40.

36   "The day of deflation approaches": Ibid., 139.

36–37   "Germany has in effect engaged . . . heaven help us all": John

Maynard Keynes, *The Economic Consequences of the Peace* (1920), 167–168, 225, 235–236, 250–251, 267–268.

37 "The existence of the great war debts": Ibid., 279.

37–38 "The immediate task": Chandler, *Benjamin Strong*, 141–142.

38 "We now hold one-half": Ibid., 266.

39 "We have had a dangerous speculation . . . over the speculator": Ibid., 329–330.

39–40 "Every situation like the present one . . . not dare to prophesy": Ibid., 428.

40–41 "This bill proceeds": Ibid., 264–265.

41 "The problem now . . . less likely to arise": Ibid., 461–462.

3. Skulls and Bones: 1929–1944

42 "You're sitting on a volcano": Bernard M. Baruch, *Baruch: The Public Years* (1960), 223.

44 "The present crisis": Allan H. Metzler, *A History of the Federal Reserve: Volume 1, 1913–1951* (2003), 279.

44 "I almost went down on my knees": Chernow, *The House of Morgan*, 323.

44 "Increased restrictive duties would be a mistake": *New York Times*, May 5, 1930.

45 "Well, Felix, this will elect me": Donald J. Lisio, *The President and Protest: Hoover, Conspiracy, and the Bonus Riot* (1974), 285.

46 "There's nothing like keeping the name": Blanche Wiesen Cook, *Eleanor Roosevelt* (1992), 1:167.

47 "I realize that if these declarations are made": H. W. Brands, *Traitor to His Class: The Privileged Life and Radical Presidency of Franklin Delano Roosevelt* (2008), 301.

47–48 "The only thing we have to fear . . . and action now!": Roosevelt inaugural address, March 4, 1933, Public Papers of the Presidents, American Presidency Project, http://www .presidency.ucsb.edu/ws/index.php?pid=14173 (accessed August 20, 2010).

48 "the withdrawal or transfer in any manner": Proclamation 2039, March 6, 1933, ibid., http://www.presidency.ucsb.edu/ws/index .php?pid=14661 (accessed August 20, 2010).

50 "After all, there is an element": Roosevelt radio address,

March 12, 1933, ibid., http://www.presidency.ucsb.edu/ws/
index.php?pid=14540 (accessed August 20, 2010).

50–52 "Nobody knows ... or the other": Roosevelt press conference,
March 8, 1933, ibid., http://www.presidency.ucsb.edu/ws/index
.php?pid=14672 (accessed August 20, 2010).

52–53 "If we are to succeed": *Foreign Relations of the United States*,
1933, 1:637.

53 "I felt almost physically ill": Raymond Moley, *After Seven Years*
(1937), 219.

53–54 "The world will not long be lulled": Roosevelt wireless message, July 3, 1933, Public Papers, http://www.presidency.ucsb
.edu/ws/index.php?pid=14679 (accessed August 20, 2010).

54 "America is the bonfire boy": Brands, *Traitor to His Class*, 371.

54 "I have rarely seen a man": Moley, *After Seven Years*, 263.

54 "It's a lucky number ... really be frightened": Arthur M.
Schlesinger Jr., *The Age of Roosevelt: The Coming of the New
Deal* (1958), 241.

55 "A rise in prices is essential": Ibid., 238.

55 "The recent gyrations of the dollar": *New York Times*,
December 31, 1933.

55 "Congratulate me": Jonathan Alter, *The Defining Moment:
FDR's Hundred Days and the Triumph of Hope* (2007), 285.

55 "This is the end of Western civilization": William E. Leuchten-
burg, *Franklin D. Roosevelt and the New Deal* (1963), 50–51.

56 "It is simply incredible ... between these extremes":
Schlesinger, *Age of Roosevelt*, 201–202, 247.

56–57 "Ever since last March ... commodity price level": Roosevelt radio address, October 22, 1933, Public Papers, http://
www.presidency.ucsb.edu/ws/index.php?pid=14537 (accessed
August 20, 2010).

58 "He was like the fairy-story prince": Moley, *After Seven Years*, 192.

4. The View from Mount Washington: 1944–1963

61 "It concerns the basis": *New York Times*, July 2, 1944.

61–62 "I hope that this conference": Ibid.

62 "Last night the American delegation": *New York Times*, July 5,
1944.

62–63   "Keynes thought that the pressure": Dean Acheson, *Present at the Creation* (1969), 83.

64   "to promote exchange stability": *New York Times*, July 23, 1944.

66   "If we do not do that": H. W. Brands, *The Devil We Knew: Americans and the Cold War* (1993), 10–11.

67–68   "Machinery has fallen into disrepair . . . desperation, and chaos": Marshall speech, June 5, 1947, http://en.wikisource.org/wiki/The_Marshall_Plan_Speech (accessed August 20, 2010).

71   "Nothing justifies double-crossing us": H. W. Brands, *The Specter of Neutralism: The United States and the Emergence of the Third World, 1947–1960* (1989), 280.

72   "We meet a brick wall": Diane B. Kunz, *The Economic Diplomacy of the Suez Crisis* (1991), 140.

72–73   "For the past decade . . . the outflow of gold": Kennedy special message, February 6, 1961, Public Papers of the Presidents, American Presidency Project, http://www.presidency.ucsb.edu/ws/index.php?pid=8178 (accessed August 20, 2010).

73–74   "The problems posed": Kennedy to Rockefeller, July 6, 1962, ibid., http://www.presidency.ucsb.edu/ws/index.php?pid=8759 (accessed August 20, 2010).

5. *Floating, Floating* . . . : 1963–1973

75–76   "American imperialism . . . This cannot last": Francis J. Gavin, *Gold, Dollars, and Power: The Politics of International Monetary Relations, 1958–1971* (2004), 117, 121.

76   "We consider it necessary": *New York Times*, February 5, 1965.

76   "Many global companies . . . unassailable by definition": Gavin, *Gold, Dollars, and Power*, 123.

76   "To go back to a system": U.S. Senate Committee on Banking and Commerce, *Hearings on S. 1307* . . . (1968), 32.

76   "The United States will continue": Johnson statement, November 18, 1967, Public Papers of the Presidents, American Presidency Project, http://www.presidency.ucsb.edu/ws/index.php?pid=28557 (accessed August 21, 2010).

77   "They will perform the same basic function": Johnson message to Congress, April 30, 1968, ibid., http://www.presidency.ucsb.edu/ws/index.php?pid=28825 (accessed August 21, 2010).

77 "Foreigners are out to screw us": Melvin Small, *The Presidency of Richard Nixon* (2003), 208.

78 "The dollar may be our currency": Peter B. Kenen, *Managing the World Economy* (1994), 36.

78 "This could be the most important weekend": William Safire, *Before the Fall: An Inside View of the Pre-Watergate White House* (2005 ed.), 510.

78–79 "There are to be absolutely no calls . . . and great courage": Richard Reeves, *President Nixon: Alone in the White House* (2001), 356–357.

79 "These actions will electrify the world . . . kick our balls off": Ibid., 357–358.

79–80 "Everybody who speculates": Safire, *Before the Fall*, 515.

80 "I want this kept secret . . . on the money market": Reeves, *President Nixon*, 358–359.

80 "Let me lay to rest": Safire, *Before the Fall*, 523.

80–81 "The time has come . . . behind her back": Nixon address, August 15, 1971, Public Papers, http://www.presidency.ucsb .edu/ws/index.php?pid=3115 (accessed August 21, 2010).

82 "Bretton Woods came at a time": Nixon news conference, December 18, 1971, ibid., http://www.presidency.ucsb.edu/ws/ index.php?pid=3268 (accessed August 21, 2010).

6. Petrodollars, Eurodollars and the Invincible Yen: 1973–1989

85 "We feel this to be a historic occasion": Daniel Yergin, *The Prize: The Epic Quest for Oil, Money and Power* (1992), 567.

85 "What is the point": Ibid., 595.

85–86 "We weren't bidding just for oil": Ibid., 615.

86 "We are heading toward the most acute shortages": Nixon address, November 7, 1973, Public Papers of the Presidents, American Presidency Project, http://www.presidency.ucsb.edu/ ws/index.php?pid=4034 (accessed August 21, 2010).

87–88 "I want to talk to you": Carter address, July 15, 1979, ibid., http://www.presidency.ucsb.edu/ws/index.php?pid=32596 (accessed August 21, 2010).

89 "Mr. Volcker has broad economic and financial experience": Carter statement, July 25, 1979, ibid., http://www.presidency .ucsb.edu/ws/index.php?pid=32648 (accessed August 21, 2010).

89 "The evening went well": Howard M. Wachtel, *The Money Mandarins* (1990 ed.), 82–83.

91 "Down five-oh-eight . . . a lot of pain": Alan Greenspan, *The Age of Turbulence* (2007), 105–106.

92 "The Federal Reserve": *Washington Post*, October 21, 1987.

7. Bubble and Boil: 1990–2002

96 "I'm the one who won't raise taxes": Bush acceptance speech, August 18, 1988, Public Papers of the Presidents, American Presidency Project, http://www.presidency.ucsb.edu/ws/index .php?pid=25955 (accessed August 21, 2010).

96 "Read my lips: I lied": *New York Times*, June 29, 1990.

97–98 "Even rising productivity . . . contemplate the world": Alan Greenspan, *The Age of Turbulence* (2007), 174–176.

98 "The stagflation of the 1970s . . . into monetary policy?": Greenspan address, December 5, 1996, Federal Reserve Board website, http://www.federalreserve.gov/boarddocs/ speeches/1996/19961205.htm (accessed November 14, 2009).

99 "And the bull charged on": Greenspan, *Age of Turbulence*, 178.

99–100 "vein of gold . . . history of the planet": David A. Kaplan, *The Silicon Boys and Their Valley of Dreams* (1999), 16–18.

100 "We will reduce taxes": Bush inaugural address, January 20, 2001, Public Papers, http://www.presidency.ucsb.edu/ws/index .php?pid=25853 (accessed August 22, 2010).

100 "I believe it's an important principle": Bush remarks, February 5, 2001, ibid., http://www.presidency.ucsb.edu/ws/index .php?pid=45826 (accessed August 22, 2010).

102 "Today we have launched a strike": Bush statement, September 24, 2001, ibid., http://www.presidency.ucsb.edu/ws/index .php?pid=64040 (accessed August 22, 2010).

102–103 "For years": Council on Foreign Relations news release, October 17, 2002, http://www.cfr.org/publication/5088/us _approach_to_curtail_money_flow_to_terrorists_inadequate _concludes_councilsponsored_independent_task_force .html?id=5088 (accessed November 15, 2009).

103 "Opium is their financial engine": *New York Times*, April 29, 2009.

104–105 "I'm going to start . . . for the euro": *Washington Times*,

January 2, 2002; *Ottawa Citizen*, January 8, 2002; *Wall Street Journal*, January 2, 2002; *Irish Times*, January 4, 2002.

105 "The purpose of the currency redesign . . . in the plans": Press release, June 20, 2002, Federal Reserve Board website, http://www.federalreserve.gov/boarddocs/press/other/2002/20020620/default.htm (accessed November 13, 2009).

106–107 "If there's anywhere in the world . . . safer and better": *Washington Post*, January 25, 1996.

8. Be Nice to Your Creditors: 2003–

109 "It's China's World": *Fortune*, October 8, 2009.

112 "What Happens When Greenspan Is Gone?": *Wall Street Journal*, January 5, 2000 (coauthored with Frederic S. Mishki and Adam S. Posen).

112 "Deflation: Making Sure It Doesn't Happen Here": Bernanke address, November 21, 2002, Federal Reserve Board website, http://www.federalreserve.gov/BOARDDOCS/SPEECHES/2002/20021121/default.htm (accessed November 12, 2009).

113–114 "It felt like there was no ground . . . an economy on Monday": *New York Times*, October 2, 2008; John Cassidy, "Anatomy of a Meltdown," *New Yorker*, December 1, 2008; and James B. Stewart, "Eight Days," *New Yorker*, September 21, 2009.

114–115 "Our system of free enterprise": Bush address, September 19, 2008, http://www.cfr.org/publication/17284/bushs_speech _on_the_financial_crisis_september_2008.html (accessed August 22, 2010).

116–119 "Does America wonder . . . the other side": James Fallows, "Be Nice to the Countries That Lend You Money," *Atlantic Monthly*, December 2008.

120–121 "Ben S. Bernanke doesn't know . . . more risk-management controls": *Wall Street Journal*, December 4 and 5–6, 2009.

121 "Doing the prudent thing": *Economist*, November 21–27, 2009.

121 "Requiem for the Dollar": *Wall Street Journal*, December 5–6, 2009.

≡ ACKNOWLEDGMENTS ≡

The author would like to thank Mark Crispin Miller, the editor of the Discovering America series, for suggesting a book about the dollar; Theresa May and Victoria Davis of the University of Texas Press for making the production process a pleasure; and my colleagues and students for letting me test my ideas on them.

≡ INDEX ≡

Acheson, Dean, 63, 66
adjustable-rate mortgages, 110
Afghanistan, 101, 112, 122
Agricultural Adjustment Act, 55
AIG (American International
    Group), 113
Aldrich, Nelson, 31–32
Aldrich, Winthrop, 56
al-Qaeda, 101–103
American Revolution, 4–5, 9
Arab-Israeli War, 85–86
atomic bomb, 65
Australia, 8

Bank of England, 38
Bank of the United States, 5–7
Baruch, Bernard, 42, 56
Bear Stearns, 111
Bernanke, Ben, 112–114, 117,
    120–122
Biddle, Nicholas, 6–7, 34
Bin Laden, Osama, 102
Black Friday, 15
Bland-Allison Act (1878), 17

Bretton Woods Conference
    (1944), 2, 60–65, 76, 117, 122;
    Eurodollars, 93; and General
    Agreements on Tariffs and
    Trade, 67; Lyndon Johnson,
    77; Richard Nixon, 81–82, 84
Britain, 47, 70–72; Bretton
    Woods Conference, 62–63;
    Franklin Roosevelt, 53; and
    gold standard, 8, 50; interest
    rates, 39–40; launch of the
    euro, 103–104; Smithsonian
    agreement (1971), 83; World
    War I, 34–36, 38; World War
    II, 58–59
Bryan, William Jennings, 20–22,
    98
Burns, Arthur, 79
Bush, George H. W., 95–97
Bush, George W., 100–102,
    114–115

California Gold Rush, 8
Canada, 8, 45, 82

Carlisle, John, 19
Carnegie, Andrew, 25, 30
Carter, Jimmy, 87–89
Central America (ship), 9
Central America, 8
Chase, Salmon P., 9–11, 16
China, 2, 59, 93, 109–110;
   investments in U.S., 115–118,
   121–22
Civil War, 1, 9, 14, 19, 35, 56
Clay, Henry, 6
Cleveland, Grover, 18–19, 22
Clinton, Bill, 97
Coinage Act (1792), 4–5, 120
Coinage Act (1873), 17
Cold War, 68, 70, 92–93, 95, 106
Common Market, 69, 103–104
Communism, 3, 68, 95, 115
Connally, John, 77–79, 81
Continental Congress, 4–5
credit-default swaps, 111
Crime of '73 (1873), 17

Davis, Jefferson, 9
Davison, Henry, 31
Dawes, Charles, 40
De Gaulle, Charles, 75–76
derivatives, 111, 116–117
dólar (Spanish currency), 4
dot-com boom, 99–100, 119
Douglas, Lewis, 55
Dow Jones, 91
Drew, Daniel, 13

Eden, Anthony, 71
Eisenhower, Dwight, 70–72
Emancipation Proclamation, 1
Emergency Banking Act, 49
euro (currency), 104–105, 108,
   121

Eurodollars, 92, 93
European Economic Commu-
   nity. *See* Common Market
European Recovery Program, 67
European Union, 104

Fallows, James, 116–118
Fannie Mae, 113
Farmers Alliance, 17
Federal Constitution of 1787,
   4–5
Federal Open Market
   Committee, 92
Federal Reserve, 1–2; Alan
   Greenspan, 90–92, 97–99;
   al-Qaeda, 102; Arthur Burns,
   79; economic crisis of 2008,
   112–113; establishment of,
   32–33; Franklin Roosevelt,
   49; globalization, 120, 122;
   Paul Volcker, 88–90; post-
   World War I interest rates, 41;
   redesign of the dollar (2002),
   105; stock market crash of
   1929, 43–44; and World War I,
   34–36, 39
Federal Reserve Act, 32, 44
Fisk, Jim, 14–15
Fort Sumter, 9
France, 34–36, 38, 40, 51, 53, 58,
   62, 70–71, 76
Frankfurter, Felix, 45
Freddie Mac, 113

General Agreements on Tariffs
   and Trade, 66–67
Germany, 2, 83, 90, 118; Bretton
   Woods, 62, 64; gold standard,
   50; post-World War I, 40;
   reunification, 95; Treaty of

Versailles, 36; *Wirtschafts-wunder* 68–69; and World War I, 34; World War II, 58–59

Glass, Carter, 32

gold, 2, 93, 98; and the dollar, 10–15, 64; Franklin Roosevelt, 54–57; Gold Rush, 8; John Kennedy, 73; "paper gold," 77; Richard Nixon, 80–84

Gold Reserve Act, 57

Gold Room, 13–15

gold standard, 119; American, 9, 34–35, 38, 50–51; British, 8, 39–41; international, 64, 76

Gold Standard Act of 1900, 22, 51

Gould, Jay, 14–15

Grant, James, 120

Grant, Ulysses, 13, 15–16

Great Depression, 42–50, 52, 86–87, 98, 112, 119

Great Society, 75

Greenspan, Alan, 90–92, 97–99, 110, 112

Group of Ten, 82

Haldeman, H. R., 80

Hamilton, Alexander, 5–6

Hawley-Smoot tariff, 44, 65

Hepburn v. Griswold, 16

Hoover, Herbert, 44–47

Hull, Cordell, 52–53

Hussein, Saddam, 101

India, 8, 71

International Bank for Reconstruction and Development, 63

International Monetary Fund, 63, 77

Iraq, 101, 112, 122

Israel, 71

Jackson, Andrew, 34

Japan, 2, 85, 112, 116–18, 121; post-World War II, 69–70; in World War II, 58, 62, 64; yen, 90, 93–95

Jefferson, Thomas, 6–7

Joachimsthal, Bohemia, 4

Johnson, Lyndon, 75–77, 122

Jones, Jesse, 54

J. P. Morgan Chase, 111

Kennedy, Joseph, 42, 72–75

Keynes, John Maynard, 36–37, 40, 55, 62–64

King George III, 4

Knickerbocker Trust Company, 22

Krugman, Paul, 121

Lamont, Thomas, 44

League of Nations, 52

Lee, Robert E., 13

Leffingwell, Russell, 56

Legal Tender Act, 1

Legal Tender Act of 1862, 12, 16

Legal Tender Cases (1871), 16

Lehman Brothers, 113

Lend-Lease, 59, 62

Lincoln, Abraham, 1, 9, 16

Louisiana Purchase, 10

Lovejoy, Owen, 10–11

Maastricht treaty (1992), 104

MacArthur, Douglas, 45

MacDonald, Ramsay, 54

Manifest Destiny, 7

Marshall, George, 67–69

Marshall, James, 8

Marshall, John, 6

McCain, John, 112

McCulloch v. Maryland (1819) 6
McKinley, William, 22, 98
Mellon, Andrew, 38
Mexican-American War, 8
Mexico, 4, 8
Moley, Raymond, 53–54
Morgan, J. P., 18–19, 22–32
Morgan Stanley, 117
Morgenthau, Henry, 54, 61

Nasser, Gamal Abdel, 70–71
National Economists Club, 112
National Reserve Association, 31
NATO, 69–71, 103
Nehru, Jawaharlal, 70
Newcomer, Mabel, 62
New York Stock Exchange, 91
Nikkei stock market index, 95
Nixon, Richard, 2, 77–86, 88, 119, 122
Norman, Montagu, 38–39
North American colonies, 4
North Atlantic Treaty of 1949, 69

Obama, Barack, 112, 115, 122
oil, 2, 3, 84–86, 122; embargo of 1973, 85
OPEC, 2, 84–85, 93
Owen, Robert, 32

Panic of 1873, 17
Panic of 1893, 18
Panic of 1907, 22–24
Patriot Act, 102
Paulson, Henry, 113–114, 117
Pelosi, Nancy, 114
Perot, Ross, 96
Peru, 4
Pickering, Thomas, 107
Populist Party, 18

Pujo, Arsène, 26, 30, 32

Rand, Ayn, 90
Reagan, Ronald, 89–90, 92, 95–96
Reid, Harry, 114
Resumption Act of 1873, 17
Robey, Ralph, 51
Rockefeller, David, 73–74, 111
Rockefeller, John B., 25, 30
Roosevelt, Eleanor, 46
Roosevelt, Franklin, 2, 45–59, 61–62, 65, 78, 113, 115, 119, 122
Roosevelt, Theodore, 22, 26, 45–47
Russia, 95, 107, 117

Safire, William, 78, 80
Sanders, Bernie, 120
Satterlee, Herbert, 22
Saudi Arabia, 102–103
Schengen agreement (1985), 104
Schumer, Charles, 114
Secret Service, 105
Seigniorage, 106, 108
Shelby, Richard, 121
Sherman Silver Purchase Act (1890), 18
Shultz, George, 80
Smithsonian agreement (1971), 82–83
South America, 8
Soviet Union, 59, 68, 70, 93, 104, 106
Spain, 4
Spaulding, Elbridge, 12
Specie, 5
Specie Circular of 1836, 7
standard silver, 5
Stein, Herbert, 78

Stevens, Thaddeus, 11
Strong, Benjamin, 23, 31–34,
  37–40, 42–43, 89, 92
Suez Canal, 71–72
Sumner, Charles, 12
Supreme Court, 6, 16, 35
Sutter, John, 8

Taliban, 103
Taney, Roger, 16
terrorist attacks of September 11,
  2001, 101–3, 110
Texas, 8
Texas Railroad Commission,
  84–85
thaler (German currency), 4
Thomas, Benjamin Franklin, 10
Thomas, Elmer, 55
Tito, Josip Broz, 70
Trading with the Enemy Act
  (1917), 48
Treaty of Versailles, 36
Truman, Harry, 65

United States mint, 4
Untermyer, Samuel, 26–30

Van Buren, Martin, 7
Vietnam, 70, 75
Volcker, Paul, 79–80, 88–91

War of 1812, 9
Warren, George, 54–55
White, Horace, 13
Wilson, Woodrow, 32–33, 46
Wirtschaftswunder (economic
  miracle), 68
World Bank, 63
World Trade Center, 101
World Trade Center bombing
  (1993), 101
World War I, 34–41, 59
World War II, 2, 58–59, 66, 79,
  81–82, 85–87, 92, 94, 97, 118

Xiqing, Gao, 115–118, 122